# KURNELL

Birthplace of Modern Australia

# Kurnell

## Birthplace of Modern Australia

### — A Pictorial History —

Daphne F. Salt

Clarion House

*To each of you with an inquiring mind.*

Published by Clarion House, 13 Prospect Place, Como West, NSW 2226

ISBN 0 9587717 3 1

© Daphne F. Salt, 2000

Researched and written by Daphne F. Salt
Photography and photographic reproduction by Daphne F. Salt

Typeset by Bungoona Technologies Pty Ltd, Sutherland NSW
Typeset in 12/13 Bembo, printed on Harvest Matt
Printed by Southwood Press, Marrickville, NSW

Produced in Australia 2000.
Website: http://ssec.org.au/kurnell

Cover: Sepia wash drawing titled "The First Landing Place of Captain Cook Botany Bay", by Samuel Thomas Gill (1818–1880). BY PERMISSION OF THE NATIONAL LIBRARY OF AUSTRALIA.
Frontespiece: Statue of Captain Cook in Hyde Park, Sydney. 2000. DAPHNE SALT.
Back Cover: Aerial view looking across Endeavour Heights (Captain Cook's Landing Place facing Botany Bay) to Kurnell Village and Towra Point, November 1999. DAPHNE SALT.

# Contents

Aerial view of Kurnell, 1999, showing Captain Cook Landing Place Reserve, Alpha House and Kurnell Village facing Botany Bay. Quibray Bay, Towra Point and the remnants of the sandhills are in the background. *DAPHNE SALT*

# Introduction

A treasure has been unearthed here!

With the zeal of a digger for gold, Daphne Salt has dug up this record of Australia's most historic place, where the two great captains, Cook and Phillip, first landed, first encountered Aborigines, first raised the flag, first observed a bush landscape utterly strange to them, and first took steps to explore.

It is a record that implies at once a tribute and a reproach: a *tribute* to ordinary Australians who have loved Kurnell, perceived its historical significance, and worked for its recognition; a *reproach* to successive governments that have neglected the 'birthplace of modern Australia', acquiesced in the appropriation of much of it by commercial interests, and remained woodenly aloof from compelling arguments for its rehabilitation.

Daphne Salt's book is a 'first' too – the first comprehensive analysis of a 230 year old history. It will flash a signal to high places that a change of attitude must come soon. And other signals are flashing: the decision to start Sydney's Olympic torchbearers' relay from Kurnell; the realisation too late that Olympic organisers should all along have been preparing Kurnell to receive a flood of interested visitors; the wider awareness that Kurnell, close to the centre of crowded Sydney, offers wonderful green, marine and historical attractions; and the strengthening resolve of Kurnell's neighbouring 210 thousand residents of Sutherland Shire to push their MPs and Councillors to agitate for Kurnell's recognition and rehabilitation.

Yes, recognition should surely come. And every reader of this book will be persuaded that it should come sooner rather than later.

BOB WALSHE

# Clarion Call

Oh, to be in Kurnell
now that April's there!

Why don't you come to Kurnell
and meet with folk who care
that here the history started
of Australia's nationhood?

For Cook, no less, chose Kurnell –
to land and to explore!
He diarised a paradise
with 'natives' whom he saw
all 'living in tranquillity'
with bay and beach and bush.

When Phillip's First Fleet followed
he too chose here to land
to bring eleven ships to rest
and raise the flag – on Kurnell's strand!

Yes, here it was, Australia,
you began the long ascent –
this Kurnell should be holy ground
its long neglect should end ...

Do come, then, to the Festival
on April twenty-nine
and shout with us a clarion call
'Make this a national shrine!'

BOB WALSHE

*For Kurnell's Year 2000 anniversary celebration of
Captain Cook's landing, 29th April, 1770.*

# Preface

## KURNELL – Birthplace of Modern Australia

This land Australia, termed by early mapmakers *Terra Australis Incognita,* had been rumoured long before the birth of Christ. Confucius wrote that the Chinese observed eclipses from the continent in 592BC and 553BC. The *Classic of Shan Hai* written before 338BC reports that the Chinese saw three things here – natives using the boomerang, black millet grown in the south, and the kangaroo. The Chinese brought back kangaroos for the Emperor's zoo in 338BC and again in 1320AD. The Portuguese used Marco Polo's 13th century maps, which showed *Terra Incognita.* These maps were used by Ferdinand Magellan, whose ships circumnavigated the earth, and by other explorers of the west coast such as Dirk Hartog in 1616 and William Dampier in 1699. Captain James Cook used them too, in 1770, on the great voyage that confirmed for the British Government the existence of a large southern continent.

The Kurnell Peninsula, where Cook landed, is bounded by the Pacific Ocean and Botany Bay; today it is a suburb of Sydney, Australia's first and largest city. Not only is this the place where Cook's 16 year old nephew, Isaac Smith, leapt ashore to hold the boat for the great Captain to land in dignity, but Kurnell has many other claims to historical importance. For instance, the collecting of plants there by Sir Joseph Banks and Daniel Solander marked the start of scientific study of Australian flora (the species they described still survive in the area).

Small wonder, then, that a number of prominent Australians have echoed the words of Sir Joseph Hector Carruthers MP when he described Cook's Landing Place Reserve in 1899: 'What Plymouth Rock is to America, so should this memorable but little reverenced spot be to all Australians'.

It is beyond comprehension that the 'Birthplace of Modern Australia' has been allowed to slip into relative obscurity, damaged by heavy industry, waste disposal and massive sand extraction – that, indeed, it has been ignored and mistreated throughout our nation's entire history. In any country but Australia, Kurnell would be a shrine!

Kurnell village began as a fishing outpost and has matured despite the industrial onslaught, yet it has retained a village atmosphere.

Our forefathers are enshrined in our affectionate memories. They were the history makers, and we are eternally grateful to them for their efforts and for their foresight in hoarding records. I would like to thank each of you who have shared your information about Kurnell, shared your knowledge, experiences and photographs. This book could not have been written without your help. I also thank Helen McDonald of the Sutherland Shire Library and the staff of the National Library of Australia, Canberra; the State Archives; the NSW Land Titles Office; the Dixson Galleries and Mitchell Library, the State Library of New South Wales; Ian Borham of the Captain Cook Study Unit, England; the Sutcliffe

Gallery, Whitby, England; Whitby Pictorial Archive Trust, Whitby, England; Captain Cook and Staithes Heritage Centre, Staithes, England.

I have asked the history teacher of my schooldays, Bob Walshe, to write an introduction to this pictorial coverage of Kurnell's history. In 1956 he researched and helped to organise a re-enactment of Cook's landing for Sutherland Shire Council's 50th Anniversary. Bob has never lost interest in Kurnell nor in history: in 1998 he was elected chairman of an alliance of ten organisations, the Kurnell Regional Environment Planning Council; he is also chairman of Sutherland Shire Environment Centre. His efforts in a long career have led to award of OAM for 'services to education and the environment'.

Welcome to Kurnell, the Birthplace of the Nation...

# 1  Origins

## Formation of Kurnell Peninsula

One million years ago Kurnell was an island. The Georges, Cooks and Towra Rivers converged and drained south-eastwards to reach the ocean at Bate Bay, effectively isolating from the then mainland an area that today we call Kurnell Peninsula. About 15,000 years ago, as the sea reached its present level, sediment filled the channels and forced the rivers to change their courses. The deepest section of the ancient river channel now lies 100 metres beneath the dunes of the southern end of the peninsula. Towra Point is actually a delta formation of relict mud and sand between the ancient rivers.

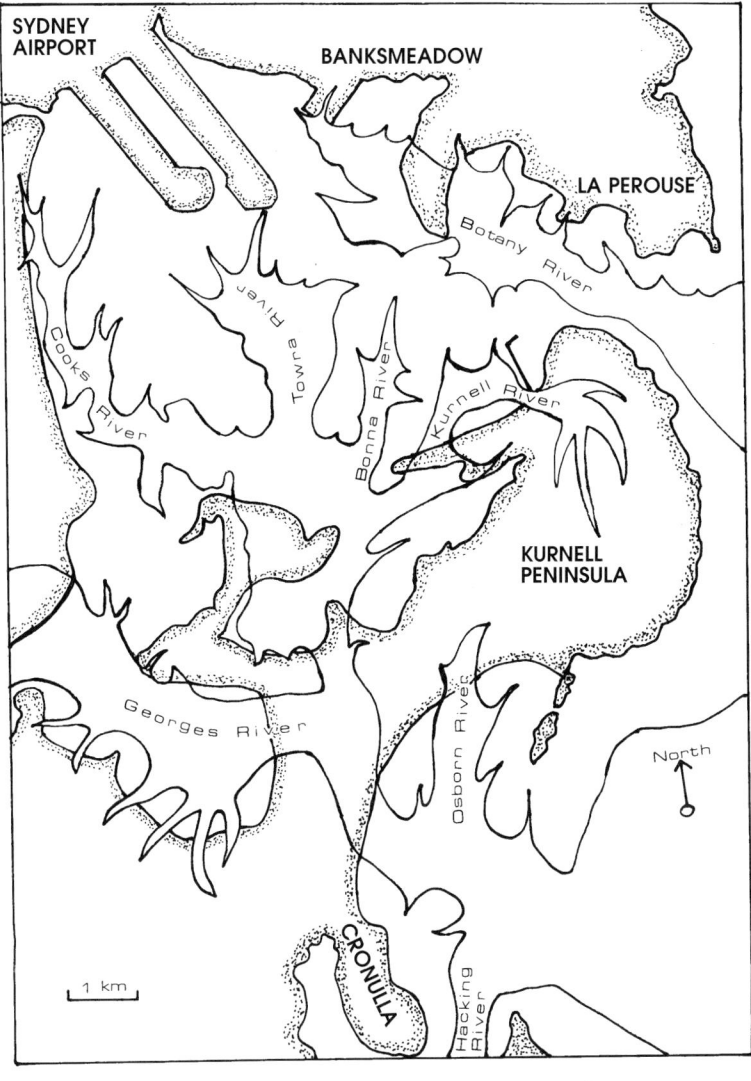

The ancient river system in relation to the Kurnell Peninsula today, sketched from geophysical reports.

## The First Australians

Aborigines migrated to Australia some 35,000 years before white man, and brought their pet dog, the dingo with them. In 1788, when the First Fleet arrived, there were an estimated 300,000 Aboriginals in Australia. In the first half of the 19th century traditional Aboriginal lifestyle quickly disintegrated. Culture, ceremonies and artefacts and were suppressed and disease reduced their numbers by more than half. By 1914 the population had declined to a mere 20,000; and it was assumed that Aborigines would eventually die out. This, thankfully, was not to be. By 1980, with the aid of improved medical services, and their own adaptation, the population of Australia's original inhabitants had swelled to about 150,000, and is soon expected to reach 300,000 again.

Anthropologists influenced administration to turn public opinion towards a more positive appreciation of Aborigines and their culture. This did not begin in Australia until 1926 and it was not until 1967 that the Australian Aborigines were given the right to vote. But despite NPWS forming a Cultural Heritage Division in 1967, the Department of Aboriginal Affairs was not established until a Tent Embassy was set up on the lawns of Parliament House in Canberra in 1972.

## Traditional Aborigines

The Australian Aborigine was a hunter and food collector. He took only what was necessary for immediate needs. He was one with and part of his natural environment and depended on it for survival. For those who place emphasis on elaborate technology and material wealth it is difficult to understand those who do not, and so neglect the complexity and richness of the Aboriginal lifestyle.

Aborigines made fire long before any contact with white man and they built rafts and canoes and they fished with spears and fishing lines.

Clothing was minimal, and consisted of a woven hair waistband in which to carry tools and weapons, and maybe, a possum-skin coat to wear in winter. The economy relied on the natural resources of the countryside. They were tradition orientated, and shared the same life-essence with all species and elements in the environment. This is the concept of the Dreamtime. The whole land was sacred with special sites of specific importance. Aborigines were the religious (spiritual) and occupational guardians of their tribal land.

In Aboriginal Australia, children grow up accepting tribal custom unquestionably. Pregnant women talk to their babies in the womb, telling

H.K.Browne's drawing of Aborigines in a bark canoe, 1819. Note the smoke from a fire in the canoe. *DIXSON GALLERIES, STATE LIBRARY OF NEW SOUTH WALES*

them of folklore, customs, family histories, myths; and they speak to the infant from the day it is born. Children grow up learning their culture in day to day conversation. Discipline for the children is maintained within the family. For breaches of Sacred Law, ritual leaders, the Tribal Council, decide on the appropriate punishment and for significant breaches there would be a gathering of many tribes at special punishment grounds.

Traditional custom is a powerful factor. Oral history, spiritual matters, myths and gossip songs are told around the evening campfire within a clan, or with a corroboree when there was a gathering of tribes. Drawings and paintings relay tribal or religious customs, depict food availability, display items available for trading (like an advertising notice board), or are done just to pass the time.

## The Kurnell Aborigines

A typical Aboriginal tribe (gal) consisted of about 20 to 50 kinsmen living in their own territory and speaking their own dialect. Eora people, from the Port Jackson region (known as Cadigal) spoke a language distinctly different from the Dharawal whose territory extends from Kurnell Peninsula to Nowra in the south and west to Camden. The Aborigines of Kurnell were the Gweagal people, and according to Beryl Timbery-Beller, Elder of the Gweagal people today – Dharawal is like a state; Gweagal is like a shire within the state; Cunnel (Kurnell) is a family village within the shire. There was no written language and it was the dialect that distinguished the separate tribes. The Gweagal Aborigines hunting, gathering and above all fishing around the southern shores of Kamay (Botany Bay) and the Georges River were the most northern tribes of the Dharawal-speaking people. They lived well from their abundant living pantry of plants, animals and seafood. They fished, using barbed spears and fishing lines with hooks, from the shore or from rafts and canoes. The abundance of fish and other foodstuffs in these heavily timbered waterways meant that these natives were less nomadic than those of inland Australia were. The numerous middens, rock carvings and paintings in the region confirm this.

*Left.* Aboriginal fish hooks made from shells. *Right.* Awl, made from a dolphin jaw bone, was used to shape the hooks which were then sharpened with a piece of ironstone. *FRED MCCARTHY*

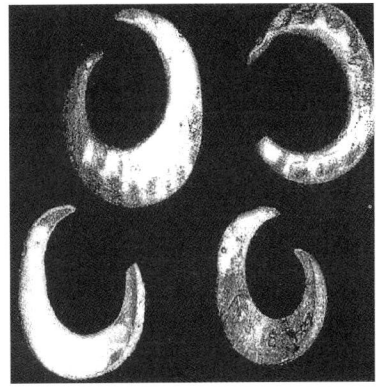
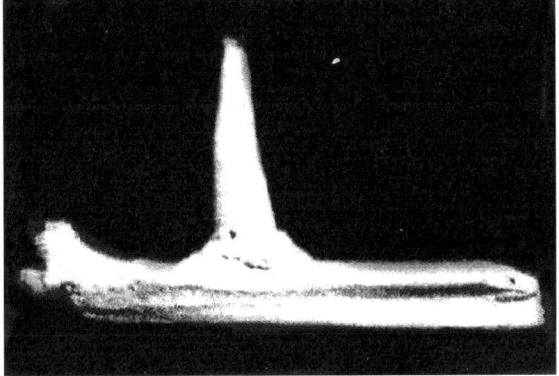

Sketch of an Aborigines making spears in front of a grass hut at the time of Cook's Landing 1770. The camp is set among banksias, eucalypts and grass trees. *MITCHELL LIBRARY, STATE LIBRARY OF NEW SOUTH WALES*

The Kurnell Aborigines were the guardians of the sacred white clay pits on their territorial land. 'Aborigines would walk hundreds of miles to get that white clay, it was *so* sacred!' The white clay had a multitude of uses – it was used to line the bottom of the canoes to make a base for the fires and it was used as the white body paint Cook wrote of witnessing. The clay was tinted with berries to produce brightly coloured paint for ceremonies and corrobories. It was eaten as a medicine – an antacid, and it was mixed with geebungs and other local berries and eaten as a dietary supplement – this clay contains zinc! Through the years its use has evolved and it is reported to still be the best white cleaner there is for tennis shoes. Even today, according to descendents of the clan, 'Aboriginal women get the cravings for that white clay when they're pregnant.'

The Aborigines called Botany Bay *Kamay,* and the Aboriginal name for Kurnell was pronounced by the Aborigines *Cunnel*. Places were often named after longstanding families. *Cundlemong* (pronounced Cunnelmong) was the last full-blood Kurnell born elder, a chief, and according to today's Aborigines the name Cundlemong was a family name and that name could be a thousand years old, passed down the line. This appears to have been corrupted by the whites to *Colonel*. It is thought that Thomas Holt combined the two words to make *Kurnell,* though Margery Hutton Neve wrote that the word might be a corruption of the native pronunciation of an early settler's name – Connell.

Cook's Cottage, Marton-in-Cleveland, by Ian Croden. This was the two-roomed, mud-walled, thatch-roofed cottage in which James Cook was born on 27th October 1728. It was demolished in 1786. *REPRODUCED WITH PERMISSION OF THE ARTIST'S WIDOW*

## Captain James Cook

Cook was born on 27th October 1728 in a two–roomed, mud–walled thatched cottage on the estate of Marton Hall in Middlesborough, North Yorkshire, England. His family later moved to Aireyholme Farm on the outskirts of Great Ayton where his father took up the position of manager. He attended the school in Great Ayton while working on the farm.

James was almost seventeen when he walked to Staithes to begin his first job, in the village general store. Eighteen months later a love of the sea drove him to the Port of Whitby and to an apprenticeship with John Walker on coal-carrying boats.

In 1755 he made the momentous decision to volunteer for the Royal Navy. Europe was arming itself for what was to become the 'Seven Years War' (1756-63). Incredibly, only one week after signing up, Able Body Seaman James Cook's abilities were recognised and he was promoted to the position of Master's Mate on board the *Eagle*. After sorting out the tangled maze of square-rigging on the near derelict ship Cook was promoted to Boatswain (Bo's'n) and sent on the *Eagle* to patrol the Bay of Biscay for French ships. During the next two years Cook saw many sea battles and his skills did not go unnoticed. He was offered the position of Master, but apologetically turned it down, opting instead to attend the Naval Academy, where he gained his Master's certificate in 1757.

A granite urn marks the site of Cook's birthplace cottage, photographed in 1995 on the 267th anniversary of Cook's birth. *DAPHNE SALT*

As a non-commissioned Warrant Officer, Master James Cook charted the St Lawrence River in 1759 and his excellent charts were a significant factor in enabling the British to take Quebec from the French. While on naval manoeuvres in Newfoundland he met a wealthy young traveller, Joseph Banks, who was later to bring him to the notice of powerful people. Cook married in 1762; he fathered five sons and one daughter, all of whom predeceased him.

In May 1768 Cook was appointed by the Admiralty to command a converted Whitby 'coal cat', renamed the *Endeavour Bark,* to voyage to the Southern Hemisphere in order to observe the transit of the planet Venus across the sun and then to look for the rumoured South Pacific continent.

He set sail from Plymouth Steps in July 1768, rounded Cape Horn in April 1769, and recorded the transit of Venus in June 1769. That done he mapped New Zealand before crossing the Tasman Sea and sighting what would become Victoria on 19th April 1770. Heavy weather conditions prevented him from landing, so he sailed on until Sunday 29th April (ship's time) when he entered Botany Bay.

## Cook In Botany Bay

On Saturday 28th April 1770, Cook wrote: 'At day light in the morning we discovered a Bay [Botany Bay] which appeared to be tollerably well sheltered from all winds and into which I resolved to go with the Ship and with this view sent the Master in the Pinnacle to sound the entrance while we kept turning up

'What Plymouth Rock is to America, so should this memorable spot on the south shore of Botany Bay be to all Australians. Not since Columbus had such a discovery been made. Birthplace though it is of the great nation that Australia is destined to be, it is comparatively little known, and certainly little reverenced. The administrative methods of the early colonial authorities allowed this, above all places, to be one of the first to pass from the Crown into private hands.' (From a booklet by the Immigration and Tourist Bureau, *Kurnell the Birthplace of Australian History*, April 1909.)

Plymouth Steps, England, in 1995. The Pilgrim Fathers on board the *Mayflower* sailed from here in 1620 bound for America, and called their Landing Place 'Plymouth Rock'. James Cook on board the *Endeavour* also set out from Plymouth Steps, in 1768, and discovered eastern Australia. *DAPHNE SALT*

with the Ship haveing the wind right out'. When Cook came to the heads of Botany Bay at 6am that morning it was low tide, and the Master sounded the entrance as the tide was rising. The tide was high when, as they ate their midday meal, they watched the Aborigines on the shore and fishing from their canoes in the bay. Joseph Banks wrote '…we soon saw about 10 people, who on our approach left the fire and retird to a little emminence where they could conveniently see our ship; soon after this two Canoes carrying 2 men each landed on the beach … the men hauled up their boats and went to their fellows upon the hill … We came to anchor abreast of a small village consisting of about 6 or 8 houses … an old woman followed by 3 children came out of the wood … when she came to the houses 3 more younger children came out … four canoes came in from fishing, the people landed [and] hauld up their boats'.

As two of the ship's boats approached the shore all but two of some thirty Aborigines who retreated to the bushes. Descendants of those Aborigines who lived at Kurnell and witnessed Cook's landing emphatically claim that their people did not run away and hide. Beryl Timbery-Beller recalls: 'When they saw a big white bird sailing into the Bay, that's what was handed down to me, they saw this big white bird coming, these two Aborigines went down as a warning party to let them get the children and hide them! They stood their ground and the others were [in the bushes as] a back-up to protect the family groups. On the rock stood two warriors, and there were about thirty marines. Two against thirty!'

Cook wrote in his journal:

> I thought that they Beckon'd to us to come ashore; but in this we were Mistaken, for as soon as We put the Boat in they again Came to oppose us upon which I fir'd a Musquet between the 2 which had no other effect than to make them retire back where bundles of thier Darts lay & one of them took up a Stone & threw at us which caused my firing a Second Musquet load with small shott, & altho' some of the Shott struck the Man yet it had no other Effect than to make him lay hold of a Shield or Target to defend himself, immidiately after this we landed which we had no Sooner done than they throw'd 2 darts at us this obliged me to fire a third Shott soon after which they both made off.

Cook's landing, as sketched in 1872. *NATIONAL LIBRARY OF AUSTRALIA*

Taking advantage of the now vacated beach Cook said: 'Isaac, you shall land first!' Sixteen-year-old Isaac Smith, cousin of Cook's wife, clambered out to hold the boat for Lieutenant James Cook to land with dignity. This beach, Milgurrung Beach, was thus the birthplace of modern Australia.

"During my stay in this harbour I caused the English colours to be displayed on shore every day, and the ship's name, and the date of the year to be inscribed upon one of the trees near the watering place." T.A. Gilfillin's painting titled 'Captain Cook taking possession of the Australian continent on behalf of the British Crown' was presented to the Philosophical Society of Victoria in 1889. Banks' greyhound is watching two men skin a kangaroo near the tent on the left of the painting. *NATIONAL LIBRARY OF AUSTRALIA*

Cook notes that when his party landed on the shore they found 'A few small hutts made of the bark of trees in one of which were four or five small children with whome we left some strings of beeds etc. A quantity of darts lay about the hutts these we took away with us.'

These huts described by Cook were made by the age-old Aboriginal technique of ringbarking a stringybark or paperbark tree at ground level and again just below the branches. The bark was then split from top to bottom and the sheet levered off and manipulated over a fire to flatten it before being left two or three days to dry. It was then laid over a frame of tied saplings. The hut was lined with the fronds of the

Thomas Medland's drawing of a Botany Bay Aboriginal dwelling in 1789. *NATIONAL LIBRARY OF AUSTRALIA*

19

Aborigines fishing with lines and cooking fish in their canoes, painted by Governor Phillip Gidley King 1790. *Mitchell Library*

cabbagetree palm for greater insulation. 'You can sleep in one of those huts in a storm and never get wet!' Beryl says.

'Three Canoes lay upon the beach the worst I think I ever saw, they were about 12 or 14 feet long made up of one piece of the bark of a tree drawn up or tied at each end and the middle kept open by means of pieces of sticks by way of thwarts'. Fish were even cooked on open fires lit on a hearth of clay in these canoes.

Able seaman Forby Sutherland, who died of tuberculosis, was buried near the watering place on May 1st. Cook named the point near his grave Point Sutherland. Sutherland was the first European to be buried in eastern Australia.

Joseph Banks recorded in his diary that each party of water–getters, grass cutters, wood gatherers and shooters from the *Endeavour* was closely observed by 12 to 15 armed natives. On one occasion '… 14 or 15 Indians having in their hands sticks that shone (say'd the Sergeant of marines) like a musquet. The officer on seeing them gathered his people together: the hay cutters coming to the main body appeard like a flight so the Indians pursued them … maybe a furlong.' The following day two of Cook's men, who had gone ashore in Weeney Bay and walked back to the camp, were chased but not attacked by 22 noisy, armed natives. In the evenings, after Cook's men had returned to the ship, at least 11

Cook's landing place photographed in 1999 from where the *Endeavour* lay at anchor. Alpha House and the refinery wharf are seen on opposite sides of the photograph.

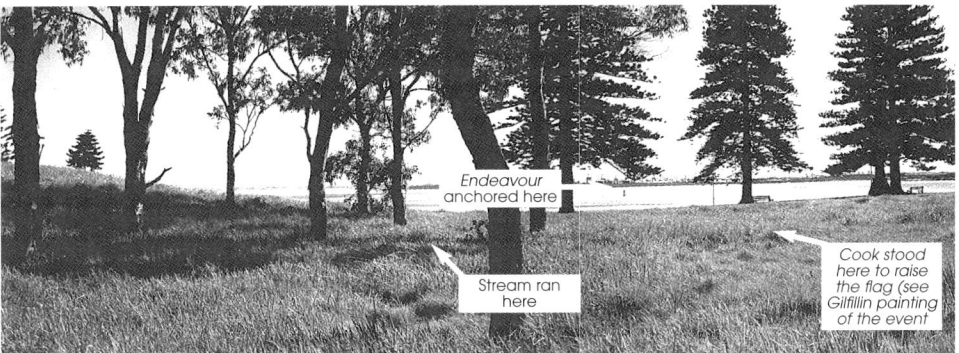

The stream from which Cook watered the *Endeavour* ran through what was then a small valley between two hills. This site was the scene of his flag- raising ceremony. The Aboriginal camp was about 100 yards to the right beside another stream in what is still a small rainforest.

canoes took to the waters of Botany Bay to catch fish, presumably because they had spent the day guarding their village.

The last full-blood Aboriginal chief of Kurnell, Cundlemong, who died in 1846 and was buried 50 metres from Sutherland's grave, said that the memory of Cook's landing was very much alive among his people.

Cook eulogised Australia as a paradise. He wrote that the Aborigines

> …may appear to some to be the most wretched people upon Earth, but in reality they are far more happier than we Europeans; being wholly unacquainted not only with the superfluous but the necessary Conveniences so much sought after in Europe, they are happier in not knowing them. They live in a Tranquility which is not disturb'd by the Inequality of Conditions. The Earth and Sea of their own accord furnishes them with all things necessary for life, they covet not Magnificent House, Household-stuff &c, they live in a warm and fine Climate and enjoy a very wholesome Air, so that they have very little need of Clothing and this they seem to be very sencible of, for many of whom we gave Cloth &c to, left it carelessly upon the Sea beach and in the Woods as a thing they had no manner of use for. In short they seem'd to set no Value upon anything of their own for any one article we could offer them; this in my opinion argues that they think themselves provided with all the necessarys of life and that they have no superfluities.

In January 1967, an archaeological excavation of one of the many middens in the vicinity of Cook's landing place at Kurnell, near Cook's stream, revealed artifacts – an axe, shell fish hooks, ironstone fish hook files, and mammal bone spear points. Well stratified in this midden was a simple bone button with a central perforation, a square-sectioned hand-made iron nail and a much-weathered portion of a glass rum bottle. Cook expressly mentions his gifts and, since carbon dating revealed the artifacts to be between 190 and 1330 years old, one may be confident that the midden was contemporary with the earliest period of white contact. The fact that these items were found in a midden buried beneath

*Banksia serrata*, one of the thousands of plants collected by Banks and Solander. Parkinson's drawing of specimens they gathered and preserved by laying the ship's sails on the ground and spreading the plants on them to dry in the sun. They took over Cook's navigational cabin and filled it with specimens. *MITCHELL LIBRARY*

successive layers of shell preserved them. Middens were Aboriginal rubbish heaps. And according to Aborigines today, they would have just thrown those things away. 'I don't think that if they threw spears at him [Cook] and got shot at, they would have valued them!', said Dharawal Elder Shayne Williams.

*Left.* Dr Daniel Solander by J. Newton. *Right.* Joseph Banks 1773, by Benjamin West. *MITCHELL LIBRARY*

During the eight days they spent in Botany Bay, Joseph Banks and Swedish naturalist Dr Daniel Solander filled the great cabin (Cook's chart and navigational room) and much of the ship's hold with botanical specimens previously unknown in Europe.

A box made from timber salvaged from the *Endeavour,* circa 1795. Until the hull sank to the bottom of Newport Harbour, the remains of the rotting ship were pillaged and made into souvenirs. *MITCHELL LIBRARY*

In 1790 the *Endeavour* was decommissioned from the navy and bought by the French, who converted her into a whaling vessel. She put into Newport, Rhode Island USA, in September 1793 with a cargo of whale oil, seeking a safe haven during the war between France and England. There she stayed until in an attempt to move her she grounded on 30th May 1794. By then she was rotten to the core. The *Endeavour* lay in Newport Harbour, disintegrating, till she was sold. The new owner dismantled her, abandoning the remains of the hull, which still lies on the bottom there. In 1996 the fragile rotten hull of the *Endeavour* was rediscovered in Newport Harbour and plans are currently under way to raise her.

A piece of timber from the *Endeavour* and one of her cannon, raised from Endeavour Reef in near perfect condition, are to be found in the Discovery Centre at Kurnell.

The First Fleet at Anchor in Botany Bay, 1788. An Aborigine in a bark canoe is seen in the foreground. *MITCHELL LIBRARY*

Lieutenant James Cook's journal records that he saw, 'The finest meadows in the world' around Botany Bay. It must have been an unusually good season. (Cook was promoted to Commander in August 1771, but he didn't officially become Captain until 1775 when he took over the Captaincy of Greenwich Hospital after he returned from his second voyage with the *Resolution* and the *Adventure.*) When Captain Arthur Phillip arrived eighteen years later with his miserable human cargo to found a convict colony, he anchored the 11 ships of the First Fleet off Bare Island on the northern side of the bay for 6 days. He had nothing kind to say about Cook's 'meadows'. According to Watkin Tench of Phillip's marines: '…we had reason to conclude the country more populace than Mr Cook thought it. For on the *Supply's* arrival in the bay on the 18th of the month [January, 1788] they were assembled on the beach of the south shore to the number of not less than forty persons, shouting and making many uncouth signs and gestures.'

Phillip immediately wrote to Lord Sydney in London explaining that Botany Bay was unsuitable for a first settlement. Nevertheless he instructed Major Robert Ross and a squad of marines to begin building wharves, clearing campsites and sinking wells near the fresh water stream on Point Sutherland. He also ordered the digging of sawpits on the headland of Cape Solander. While that was being done (closely watched by muttering, gesticulating, armed and angry Aborigines), he took three boats to an inlet to the north, named Port Jackson by Cook but not entered by him. It is now world famous as Sydney Harbour.

On January 24th, as Phillip was preparing to relocate the fleet to 'the finest harbour in the world', two French ships were sighted attempting to enter the heads of Botany Bay. Phillip sent a boat to guide them in, while he hastily had the British colours hoisted on Point Sutherland and on all his ships to signal that Britain had claimed the territory. Thus, remarkably, this territory was only days short of perhaps becoming a French colony.

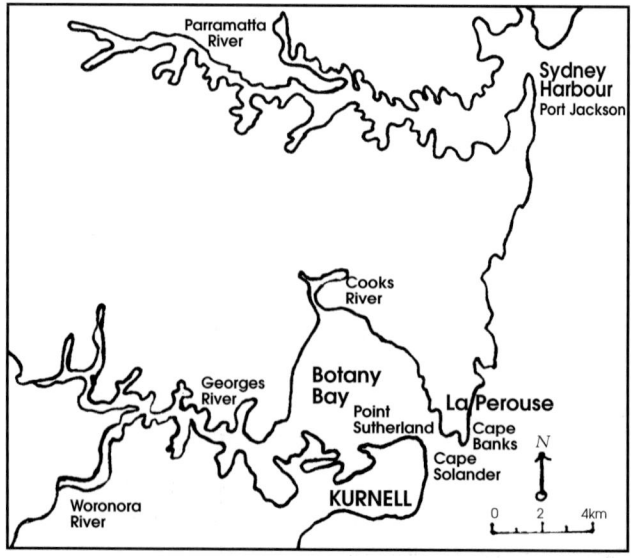

Sketch showing the relationship of Botany Bay and Port Jackson (Sydney Harbour). Point Sutherland and Cape Solander are on the Kurnell Peninsula. La Perouse, named after the leader of the French fleet that entered Botany Bay during Phillip's stay, and Cape Banks are on the northern side of the entrance to Botany Bay.

# 2  Occupying the Land

## Birnie, Connell, Laycock

Twenty seven years after the First Fleet departed from Botany Bay the first official land grant in the pre-Sutherland Shire was made to James Birnie, a merchant trader and master of a sealing and whaling sloop. In 1815, he was given, 'On Promise', Portion No.1, 700 acres of land and 160 acres of saltwater marshes. The semi-literate clerk recorded the grant as he heard it: Birnie's *Alpha Farm* (meaning 'the beginning') became *Half-A-Farm* in the official records.

Birnie intended building a whaling station there. He set up a farm, market garden and dairy and built a homestead, which he named *Curnell* (the Aboriginal name for the area as he heard it). There he installed his caretaker/manager while he pursued whaling and other shipping interests from his Sydney home.

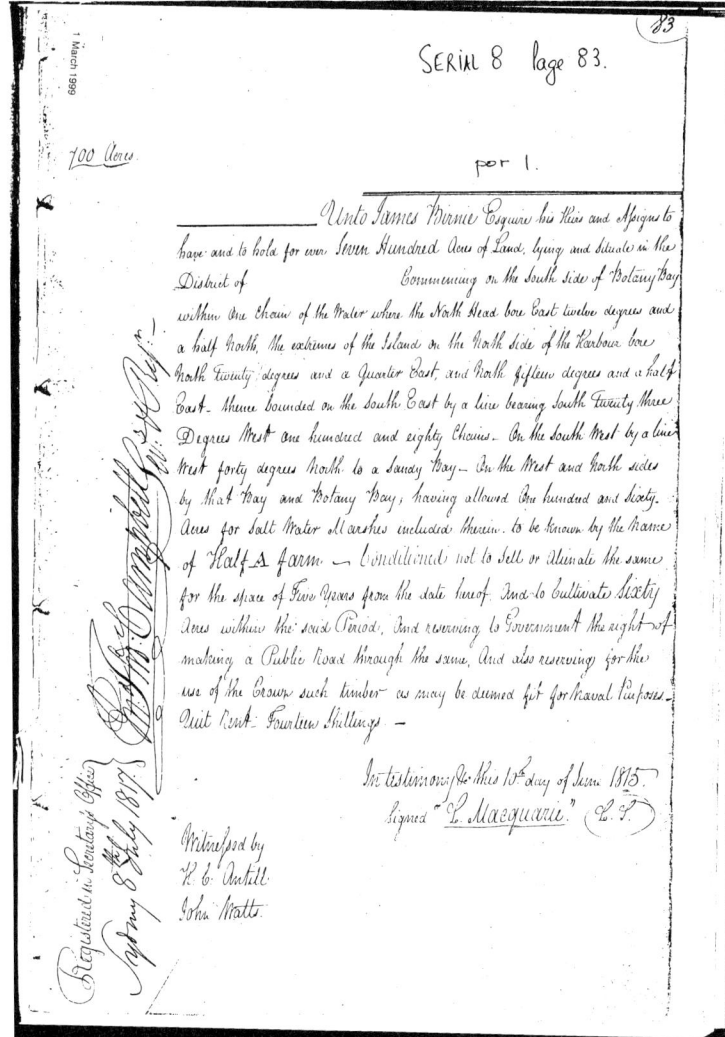

Page from the register showing details of the 'Half-A-Farm' (Alpha Farm) grant to James Birnie, 1815, registered 1817.
*NSW Land Titles Office*

In 1801 John Connell, widowed in England, came to Australia with his two children (Margaret and John), as a free settler. He transferred his London business to Sydney, setting up a large ironmongery shop where Australia Square now stands. Catherine Sullivan, a convict transported to Australia in 1798, was assigned to Connell as a servant and, after marrying him in Sydney was pardoned.

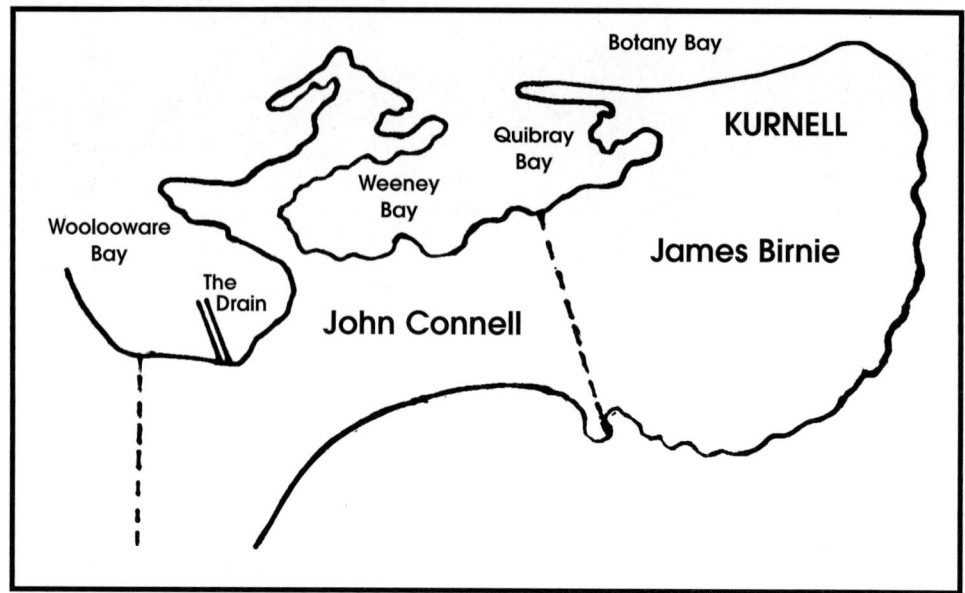

Map of land ownership on the Kurnell Peninsula, about 1821.

In 1821 Connell obtained 'On Promise' an additional 1000 acres on Quibray Bay. When the 66 year old Birnie was declared insane in 1828, the trustees of the Birnie Estate sold his land to John Connell. In the same year, Connell erected a cottage, Alpha House, on the foundations of Birnie's old three-roomed house.

Margaret Connell, who had married Captain Thomas Laycock, had two sons, Elias Pearson Laycock and John Connell Laycock. Both parents died when the boys were young, and John Connell became their guardian.

By 1838 almost the entire Kurnell Peninsula, including Birnie's 'Half-A-Farm', was in the name of John Connell. John junior lived on Alpha Farm. This Connell cleared heavily, selling the timber in Sydney. He transported ironbark, turpentine, blackbutt, mahogany and red cedar from the Hacking River and Kurnell areas to the Sydney market before the 1840s. By having a canal dug to Woolooware Bay – in the approximate position of today's mangrove boardwalk behind the Sharks Leagues Club – he was able to float the timber into Botany Bay whence his waiting ships carried it to Sydney.

When John Connell senior died in 1849 he left his entire Estate to his grandsons as tenants in common.

In 1856 the Government held the first auction of land in the Sutherland district at £1 per acre, but it reserved 1500 acres for fortifications on the east coast from Cape Solander to Boat Harbour (Endeavour Heights) and the Cronulla

Stumps of large trees exposed by a combination of weather conditions and sandmining in 1970 bear reproachful witness to the forests that were logged during the nineteenth century.
*Sutherland Library*

Peninsula. John Connell Laycock secured over 700 acres at the sale. By 1858 he owned 4500 acres and had settled again at Kurnell.

For J.C. Laycock, 1860 was a year of disaster. He had mortgaged most of his inheritance to Thomas Holt and had bought extensive properties in Sydney, Sutherland, Liverpool and Queensland. Six months after he had purchased the Prince of Wales Theatre (largest theatre in Australia at the time) and adjoining properties in Sydney, fire broke out destroying all of his buildings and killing two people. He was not adequately insured and was forced to sell all his mortgaged properties the following year. Laycock was a Member of the Legislative Assembly and a friend of fellow Member, Thomas Holt. Prior to his land sale he had shown Holt around his Hacking and Georges River properties.

## Thomas Holt

Thomas Holt was born in Yorkshire in 1811, the eldest of five sons of a Leeds wool manufacturer and merchant. At the age of fourteen he left school and went into his father's business. At twenty-one he left England to represent the firm in the wool markets on the Continent. Whilst in Berlin he married Sophie Eulert. It was there that he read the German translation of Dr John Dunmore Lang's *An Historical and Statistical Account of New South Wales,* a book describing the colony and its potential – it was to change his life.

In 1842 Holt and his bride sailed into Sydney. He arrived a wealthy man, and began at once to speculate in mortgages and the money market; he also obtained grants for huge tracts of Colonial Crown Land. He amassed vast sums of money by disposing of his squatting holdings throughout the State during the flurry of land sales following the gold discoveries in the early 1850s. A city man, he nevertheless delighted in being the Country Squire, but always held country

Executive Council of the first Responsible Government of NSW, 1856. Thomas Holt, Colonial Treasurer; Sir William Manning, Attorney-General; Sir Stuart Donaldson, Colonial Secretary; J.B. Darvall, Solicitor-General; George Nichols, Auditor-General. *MITCHELL LIBRARY*

estates (on Botany Bay and its tributaries) close enough to commute into Sydney to his counting house, so maintaining control over his business affairs. Holt was a member of the first New South Wales Legislative Assembly (1856) He became the first Treasurer in what was in fact Australia's first Parliament.

Holt owned land in Queensland as well as his extensive holdings throughout New South Wales. He built six mansions to the south of Sydney, Sutherland House at Sylvania being the last he built.

At the 1861 auction of Laycock's land, Holt was the highest bidder at £3275 for the entire 4600 acres. Amongst the properties bought by Holt was the Birnie

Sutherland House, overlooking the Georges River at the mouth of Gwawley Bay (now Sylvania Waters), contained 39 bedrooms, each with a view over the water. Built in 1871, it was destroyed by fire December 1918. *CLARA RICE*

Thomas Holt MLA, 1879. *Mitchell Library*

Estate, which comprised all of the Kurnell Peninsula with the exception of the Government Reserve at Endeavour Heights, and included the Landing Place of Cook. The 4600 acres Holt bought from Laycock were scattered lots. During 1861-62 he consolidated his holdings by securing large portions of land between the Georges and the Hacking Rivers. He even procured two waterways – Gwawley Bay and Weeney Bay. His accumulated holdings in the pre-Shire were approximately 13000 acres.

Thomas Holt, with a view to economics, procured the services of government men (convicts), runaway sailors and Aborigines for the workforce on his estates. Although he had the former Connell overseer, Mr Justice, living on-site at Kurnell, Holt employed a Gweagal Aborigine, William Rowley, born at Pelican Point (Towra Point) in 1831, as his foreman.

Aboriginal workers on the Holt Sutherland Estate, 1880. Jim Brown (uniform) known as 'Jimmy the loafer'; Joe Brown (back, wearing dark coat); Joey a tribal Elder and brother to Biddy Giles; Biddy Giles, widow of 'King Kooma' the last king of the Georges River tribe, (after her husband died, Biddy married Englishman Billy Giles and lived on Blaxland's Old Farm); Jimmy Lowndes, expert horseman and lassoer (he drove a bullock team for Holt and was also a great athlete and deadly with a gun). *Daphne Salt*

## Holt and his Oysters

Holt began the oyster culture industry in Australia in the waters of Weeney and Gwawley Bays. In 1866 before leaving for Europe, he converted Weeney Bay into an oyster breeding ground by placing timber there to attract oyster spawn. He visited oyster culture industries in France, Italy, and England. On his return he found 'the timber was covered with oysterlings as white as snow'. He had miles of channels dug in Gwawley Bay, and had the bay's mouth enclosed with a bridge in which were flood gates to control the water flow. This was the first oyster farm in Australia. Weeney Bay was enclosed with piles. Oysterlings (immature oysters) from overseas and from Cowan Creek, Pittwater, Georges River and Port Hacking were placed there to grow before being put into Gwawley Bay claires (oyster breeding channels). Oyster leasing was officially introduced in 1880, after Holt pushed for it in Parliament.

## Violation of the Dunes

The Kurnell sand dunes were a unique and fragile phenomenon. In hollows between the dunes, small lakes and swamps formed, providing a wide range of foraging, sheltering, roosting, and breeding resources for native animals and birds and for the campsites and burial grounds of Aborigines.

When Captain Cook walked across the Kurnell headland, through its forest and scrub, to look down on what is today called Cronulla Beach, the sandhills were completely covered in healthy scrub, large trees and native grasses.

According to the handwritten 1868 Sutherland Estate Report, the Estate was still mostly virgin land covered with scrub and timber and the only grasses were the native varieties. But Holt then began an intensive project to clear and cultivate. He imported and planted grass seed that he had bought in Germany.

Remains of Holt's post and rail fence can still be found on Towra Point today.

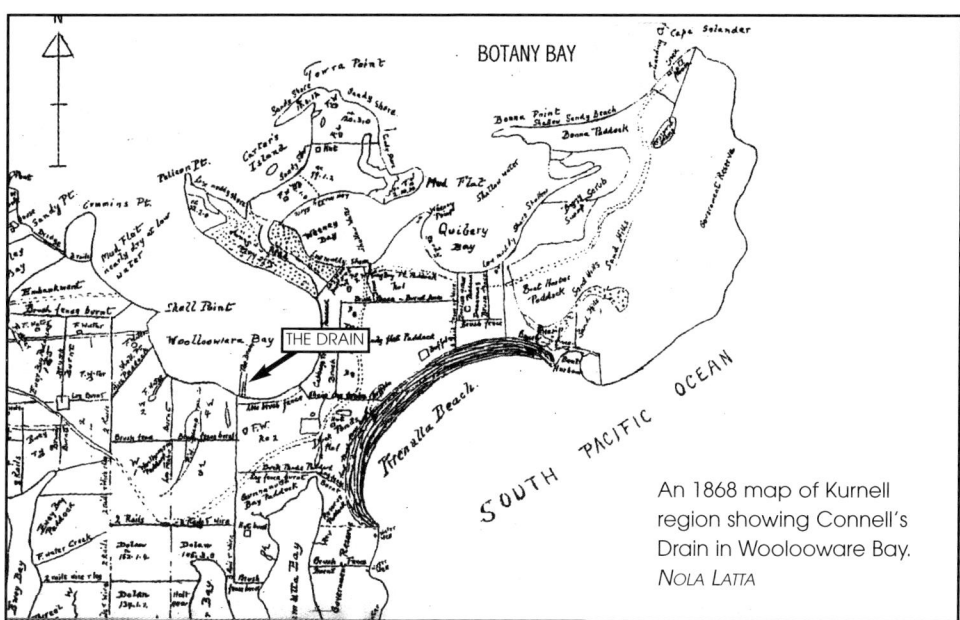

An 1868 map of Kurnell region showing Connell's Drain in Woolooware Bay.
*NOLA LATTA*

The Estate was divided into eleven paddocks using split-rail fences (the remains of some are still to be found on Towra Point), each with a water supply of some sort; these were then divided by brushwood fences to make over 60 smaller paddocks.

Adversity assailed Holt's pastoral efforts. With his grasses growing on the cleared land, he had brought in sheep. Dingoes at first killed thousands of them. One shooting party reported killing 300 dingoes. Just as he brought these wild dogs under control, he found that his sheep were infected with footrot. John Cooper Walker, Holt's Sutherland Estate manager, recorded that in 1868 he had '1300 of the infected sheep destroyed and buried at Towra Point, with a covering of seaweed to assist their decomposition and to procure fertilisation of the soil'.

Holt tried cattle next but they fared little better. The hungry cattle completed the damage the sheep had begun. In 1870 the green hills on Kurnell Peninsula showed big areas of exposed sand where the grass had been eaten out – and the bared dunes have been spreading ever since! By the turn of the century the now moving sandhills covered an extensive area. In an effort to check the damage, Holt imported buffalo grass from America to supplement the native grasses and the other foreign grasses he had planted.

In a bid to recoup his losses, Holt tried his hand in the timber industry. Turpentine, ironbark, blackbutt and mahogany were felled and floated out through Connell's canal (known as The Drain) in Woolooware Bay to his ships. Eventually Holt sold the rights to all standing timber on his property. Yet in 1873 Holt had the gall to urge the NSW Government to take immediate steps to preserve the State's timber.

Circa 1851, looking across Kurnell's vegetated dunes. *Sutherland Library*

## The Sandhills

When James Cook in 1770, had looked down on what is today called Cronulla Beach from the sandhills, which covered over 1000 acres and rose to 200 feet, he had made no mention of any bare dunes. Less than 100 years later the scrub had been cleared and burnt, the trees had been ringbarked or cut down for the timber

Cattle grazing on the dunes. Sand is beginning to be exposed because of loss of the restraining grass cover, 1860. *Mitchell Library*

Extensive areas of sand exposed because of the grazing sheep and cattle, 1870. *Fred Midgley*

industry, and Holt's grazing stock had eaten out the restraining grass cover. This intervention of man unleashed the sands to produce an unstable transgressive dune sheet that moved north at the rate of at least 8 metres a year.

Looking north along what is now Wanda Beach, towards Boat Harbour, 1895. *Fred Midgley*

Logging in Kurnell in the 1920s. SUTHERLAND LIBRARY

Paul Allan and David Salt playing on the dunes, 1978. Note the overhead power lines, near the top of the dunes, transmitting power to the Caltex Oil Refinery.

In 1933 the Sutherland Shire Council asked the Government to set aside the 2000 acres between Cronulla Golf Club and Kurnell as a reserve. But the Government could see no reason to establish another National Reserve so near to Captain Cook's Landing Place Reserve.

In 1937 the Council was offered 720 acres of sandhills at a low price. The Council was evenly split and the negative casting vote of its President, C. O. J. (Joe) Monro, foreshadowed the doom of the dunes. Since then the escalating extraction of sand for the Sydney building industry has seen in excess of 70 million tonnes of sand carted away. The once towering pristine dune-scape, a playground for generations of children, has been reduced to a few remnant dunes and deep water-filled pits, many of which are now being filled with demolition waste from Sydney's building sites.

Marcel Gorel, Ron Bussing and Ashley Boon on top of a dune; cars can be seen below, 1970. *Leni Bussing.*

1905, Boat Harbour and Bate Bay dunes. *Cronulla Surf Life Saving Club*

A scene from the movie *40,000 Horsemen*, set in the Kurnell dunes, 1938. *NATIONAL FILM AND SOUND ARCHIVES*

Because of the enormous expanse of sand and the sensation of being isolated in a remote desert region these dunes were used until the 1980s for movies such as *40,000 Horsemen, Rats of Tobruk, Thunder in the Desert, Phar Lap,* and *Mad Max – Beyond Thunderdome.*

Tower facade made of wire netting and stucco for *40,000 Horsemen,* 1938. Wal Campbell (on left) was in the Charles Chauvel film with actor Chips Rafferty. *DON CAMPBELL*

## Alpha House

Although pioneer James Birnie never lived on his grant he erected a three-roomed cottage in which his manager lived, and another smaller cottage for the servants. He was assigned convict labourers to fell the trees and clear the land. Alpha Farm was self-sufficient with its dairy and its orchard and vegetable gardens, all irrigated by water from Cook's stream. He transported the produce to Sydney markets. The manager cut a 'shipping dock' through the rock to enable the boats to come up to the grassy bank at high tide.

In 1821 Connell leased some of his land to Birnie for grazing cattle; then in 1828 when Birnie was declared 'lunatick' his trustees sold the Birnie Estate to John Connell. Connell built another cottage on the foundations of Birnie's old one but retained its underground cool rooms, which are still there. This cottage stood for a little over seventy years.

John Connell junior lived on Alpha Farm where he raised his two nephews. Later he moved to a Clarence River property leaving the boys to take care of Kurnell. After Thomas Holt bought the Laycock lands, which included Alpha Farm in 1861, Laycock's overseer, Mr Justice, who lived in Alpha House, stayed on to work for Holt.

After Mr Justice, other caretakers lived in the cottage. In 1887 Fred Beaker, Holt's caretaker and wood-getter, resided in Alpha House. He provided meals and beds for those who visited Kurnell and sought accommodation. When Beaker finally vacated the aging cottage the locals plundered it for its materials. In the 1890s, a fisherman's son was playing in the ruin and unearthed a tin pot filled with half crowns from the foundations.

News of the find proved disastrous for what was left of the old edifice. Hordes of treasure-seekers poured in and razed the house and the dairy beside it to the ground. But not another coin was found.

Two pine trees planted in John Connell's time, and the remains of the second Alpha House that was built by John Connell in 1828. Photograph by Sir Joseph Carruthers 1898. *Mitchell Library*

Land for the Captain Cook Landing Place Reserve was resumed in 1899 and in the same year it was officially opened and dedicated to the people for all time. Alpha House lay in ruins for a further year or two before the Trustees of the Reserve built another cottage on the foundations of the previous two. They retained the name Alpha House. In 1902 the Government granted £50 to the Trustees to meet expenses in connection with the official opening of the wharf and guesthouse.

The present Alpha House rebuilt on the original foundations by the Reserve Trustees in 1902. MITCHELL LIBRARY

Alpha House, photographed here in 1920, was used as a guest house. ELSIE POPPLEWELL

Alpha House from Milgurrung Beach, 1999.

Alpha House from the air, November 1999. *Daphne Salt*

# 3  The Landing Place Reserve

## Recognition of the Cook Landing Place

On 20th March 1822 an old Aborigine, 'white haired and hoary with age', who had witnessed Cook's landing, accompanied members of the executive of the Philosophical Society of Australasia to Kurnell and pointed out the landing place to them. They fixed a brass plate (to commemorate 50 years since the landing of Captain Cook) on the cliff-face a little to the north east of the Landing Place as the nearest available spot.

In 1870 Thomas Holt erected an obelisk at his own expense to celebrate the centenary of Captain Cook's landing at Kurnell.

On Saturday 8th August 1881 the two visiting royal princes, Prince Albert, Duke of Clarence, and the future king, George, Prince of Wales, travelled to Kurnell by boat from Botany. *The Sydney Morning Herald* reported:

Pencil drawing by Samuel Thomas Gill of Captain Cook's Landing Place, 1856. Alpha Farm is to the right. In 1822 the Philosophical Society fixed a tablet to the rocks east of Inscription Point to commemorate the landing. Cook landed in front of Alpha House. *National Library of Australia*

The one spot in all Australia which can claim to be called Classic Ground is undoubtedly that little area by the southern shore of Botany Bay, where, more than a century ago, Captain Cook first set foot on the soil of this continent; where the seaman Forby Sutherland was buried; and it was but right that the Royal Princes, now amongst us – one of whom will probably ascend the throne of Great Britain; should not be allowed to leave the colony without being asked to visit the scene … Nearly everyone took a sip of the water from the historic stream.

Details of the tablet that the Philosophical Society fixed to the cliffs.

1822 Philosophical Society's plaque in its second position nearer Solander than Inscription Point. *NATIONAL LIBRARY OF AUSTRALIA*

Near the obelisk, Prince Albert and Prince George planted four pine trees, one of which was *Araucaria Cookii* which Holt had brought over from New Caledonia. Cook had identified it as a separate species and Banks named it there during his voyage. The tree planting and official proceedings over, the party

Holt's obelisk with Silver Beach in background, about 1900. *CAROLINE DAVIS/WEIR*

Prince Albert and Prince George during their Australian visit, 1881. *NPWS, Kurnell*

strolled around inspecting the historic area. The princes joined a group of Kurnell residents in a game of cricket before sitting on the ground for lunch. 'A marauding dog, which had pilfered a plump turkey, was hotly pursued by the waiter; whereupon Prince Albert joined in the chase, and outpacing the waiter, made a cut with his stick at the thief. The dog dropped his prey; and the prince retrieved the bird.'

## Resumption of the Reserve

About 250 acres of land, including that on which the obelisk and Forby Sutherland's grave are situated, was resumed by the Government in 1899 and dedicated as the Captain Cook Landing Place Reserve for the use and enjoyment of the public for all time. A formal and public dedication by His Excellency the Lieutenant Governor, the Honorable Sir Frederick Darley, was to take place on the 28th April 1899 [calendar date; and 29th April by the ship's log date], being the anniversary of Captain Cook's landing. Unfortunately the state of the weather necessitated a postponement until the 6th May – the date on which Captain Cook sailed away from Botany Bay.

Steam ferries conveyed guests across Botany Bay and the party was escorted to a dais erected on the rise of the hill at the rear of the monument. After all the guests had assembled the ceremony began. The Lieutenant Governor, the Admiral and the Minister for Lands all delivered speeches. In his address Sir Joseph Carruthers, Minister for Lands, said '... this land is at last rescued from the hands of any private individual or land corporation. What blind folly ever induced the Government of New South Wales to part with this area of land for a paltry £1 per acre? It may be mere sentiment on my part to rescue this land as a national birthright!'

---

**DEDICATION**

——◦◦◦◦◦——

CAPTAIN COOK'S

Landing Place

~ At KURNELL, ~

On 28th April, 1770.

Saturday, 6th May, 1899.

Invitation to the Dedication of Captain Cook's Landing Place Reserve. *NPWS, Kurnell*

Glover's sketch of Holt's obelisk at high tide, 1878. *National Library of Australia*

## Dedication Ceremony

Sir Joseph Carruthers reminded the gathering that in 1861 twenty-year-old Henry Kendall visited Kurnell with Thomas Holt, who told the poet about his finding the bones of a white man. Fired by the significance of this discovery Kendall wrote:

> *There* tread gently – *gently,* pilgrim; *there* with youthful eyes look round;
> Cross thy breast and bless the silence: lo, the place is holy ground!
> Holy ground forever, stranger! All the quiet silver lights
> Dropping from the starry heavens thro' the soft Australian nights –
> Dropping on those lone grave grasses – come serene, unbroken clear,
> Like the love of God the Father, falling, falling, year by year!
> Yea, and like a Voice supernal, *there* the daily wind doth blow
> In the leaves above the sailor buried ninety years ago.

Tree planted by the Duke of Clarence, and Holt's wharf over what is now known as Cook's Rock. Remnants of the piers remain on that rock. *Mitchell Library*

Old post card showing visitors to the Captain Cook Landing Place Reserve in 1905 using the wharf which Thomas Holt had built. For these Cook celebrations a Sylvania punt was brought up to the wharf to be used as a floating dock for the convenience of the visitors. *RONALD CORLETTE THEUIL*

Holt's obelisk and the Isaac Smith memorial on 'Cook's Rock', 1999. *DAPHNE SALT*

*Endeavour II* in Botany Bay, 29th April 1970, for the 200th anniversary re-enactment of Cook's landing. Queen Elizabeth II officiated at this ceremony. GEORGE BLUNDELL

The *New Endeavour* in Botany Bay in on 29th April 1995 for the 225th anniversary celebrations of the landing of Captain Cook. NOELINE THOMAS

# 4 Squatters and Campers

## Tourism

In 1909 the Sydney Immigration and Tourist Bureau published a booklet stating that the Trustees of the Reserve (the Lands Department) had recently constructed a new up-to-date boat jetty and had cut a new walk, at considerable expense, through the thick natural growth, round the seafront from Inscription Point and circling back to the neighbourhood of the Trustees Cottage. They installed swings for the children, summerhouses, shelter-sheds, and other facilities for picnicking and camping parties amongst the groves of banksias. First-class accommodation for approved visitors was available at the Trustees Cottage at 8 shillings a day. On Sundays and on all public holidays the excursion steamers left from Brighton, Sans Souci, Botany Pier, and La Perouse.

Holt's obelisk and the Reserve wharf constructed by the Trustees of the Reserve in 1902.
*CAROLINE DAVIS*

## Camping in the Reserve

In 1899 a report on Kurnell revealed that the fishing was rewarding and that 'Oysters are plentiful and large and may be detached from the mangroves about Quibray Bay. Ashore there is always good shooting'. Sir Joseph Carruthers kept a careful tally of his hunting triumphs. During 1883 he shot 256 birds and animals including hawks, quail, parrots, wattlebirds, koalas and snakes. Sportsmen at the time were also shooting kangaroos and koalas.

'Koala' is an Aboriginal word meaning 'no water'. This unique, inoffensive marsupial was so named because it derives its hydration, not from drinking water, but from its diet of eucalypt leaves. In 1938 concern was expressed for the diminishing number of koalas, but in 1945 an application for a koala sanctuary at Kurnell was rejected and the consequences were fateful… There have been no koalas living at Kurnell for nearly fifty years.

*Left.* Koala. Once so prolific on the Kurnell Peninsula, koalas were shot as sport. *Right.* An heroic shooter posing with his tally of three dead koalas. CLARENCE RIVER HISTORICAL SOCIETY

Throughout the intervening years, until 1966 when the National Parks and Wildlife Service took over its care, the Reserve was one of the most popular camping venues close to Sydney. Site bookings were taken two years in advance. Under the provision of the NPWS Act 1967, the area was increased to about 700 acres by the addition of a coastal strip of land from Cape Solander to Cape Bailey. In 1968 a further 100 acres was added to the park.

## Tabbigai Cliff Dwellers

Tabbigai Cliffs, located about 1km south of Cape Solander, were home to men such as Bert Adamson, Gordon Donovan, and Sid James, who have left a record of their experiences. They lived there, happily, from the 1920s until their cliff houses were demolished in 1974. Permissive occupants at Tabbigai, not squatters, they paid an annual fee to the Lands Department and also paid Council rates for the right to occupy their precarious ledge. The trio had camped and fished from

Tabbigai cliff fishing houses "clinging to the edge of the world". The load bearing beams ran well into the sandstone of the cliff face. *MITCHELL LIBRARY*

a somewhat sheltered, wide ledge since they were in their teens. Most cliff houses such as theirs were built during the Depression years of the late 1920s and the 1930s.

During the 1930s the three fishing mates constructed a comfortable home and gradually added modern conveniences and extra rooms. They scraped, sealed

*Left.* Cliff houses at Tabbigai. *Right.* Fishing boxes beneath the walkway.

and painted the inside cave walls and extended the roof beyond the cliff face to protect them from gales and rain.

Passageways and tunnels were dug through the rock. Water came from a natural spring. They used kerosene lights and refrigerators; a generator supplied their electricity and they even carpeted their floors. Included in the complex was a guest flat! They considered themselves Australia's luckiest citizens, living in their own idea of Heaven, dropping a fishing line out of the loungeroom window to catch breakfast, lunch or dinner. The Aborigines never had it as good as this.

In 1961 the Lands Department reviewed the permissive occupancy agreements and ordered the cliff dwellers and permanent Reserve campers to leave. Two of the mates grudgingly complied while pointing out that they paid their rates to the Sutherland Shire Council; Bert, however, refused to budge and he might well have lived out his days there had it not been for vandals who set fire to a stolen car and pushed it over the cliff so that it hit the roof of the cliff house and its exploding petrol tank demolished the house in a blaze of fire, razing 40 years of idyllic existence. Bert was then 75 years old; he left reluctantly to live in highly urbanised inner Sydney.

Tabbigai was not the only cliff-face dwelling area, though it was the most substantial, the most comfortable and the most longstanding. There were camps all along the cliffs overhanging the ocean. The cliff dwellers kept an eye on the park visitors and deterred vandalism. There was one such camp at Inscription Point beside the Natural Arch where campers gouged out a little chamber about 12 inches long to catch fresh drinking water. That trough fills with fresh water to this day.

Inside one of the fishing cave dwellings at Inscription Point near the Natural Arch. *Elsie Popplewell (Honnor)*

Most of the camps in the Reserve were of a permanent nature and, like the cliff houses, were built during the Great Depression or soon after the Second World War. Thomas Holt Jnr allowed camps on his land at Boat Harbour for payment of a fee. Boat Harbour became a 'Happy Valley' shantytown. In 1922 it was reported that there were as many as fifteen humpies on one piece of land there.

Water trough gouged out beneath this stone pillar in 1930 still fills with fresh water.

The Natural Arch and fountain at Inscription Point, 1999, showing the water trough carved out at its base to supply the camping fishermen with fresh drinking water.

## Golden Years in the Reserve

Kurnell's camping heydays were undoubtedly during the 1940s and 1950s prior to the construction of the road. Lee Jones tells of her first glimpse of Kurnell:

'As we came across by ferry it was a glimpse of heaven, all lush and green. I fell in love with it! During the school holidays the women and kids stayed in the camps, the men came over on weekends with food. The camps were very comfortable; we had a kero stove, pressure lamps and a tin bath we filled with water we heated in a four-gallon drum on the primus.

'The park was a really close community of its own. The campers would all look after each other. We used to have entertainment nights in the camp, some

Ladies walking in the park in the 1930s. *Harry Morgan*

Preparing an evening meal in the Reserve camp. *LEE JONES*

would sing or tell stories making pots of tea, and coffee and toast and often the men would talk about their days on the track during the Depression. There were about 30 permanent camps, some of them on the flat where the flagpole is.

'On the Saturday night, on Latta's bus, we used to go in to Cronulla to the pictures and we'd be stuck in the sandhills two or three times and it'd be all out – everybody out and push the bus out. There was no road out to Kurnell, only a track that sometimes disappeared under the moving sandhills. When the winds were really bad we were cut off completely from Cronulla and also if the seas were very rough we couldn't get over to La Perouse to go home.

'Fieldings were the caretakers in the park. You placed your order during the week and they brought it in. The little shop was at the back of Alpha House in the park. The Field Study Centre was later built as the park shop and tea-room. Betty Fielding would bake HOT Scones for Devonshire teas with jam and fresh cream.'

'At Christmas the park would be booked out by many of the factories and businesses for day picnics and there would be people everywhere. It was a very popular spot.'

When the Reserve came under the provision of the NPWS Act in

Stan Latta's bus from Kurnell to Cronulla. *NOLA LATTA*

Betty Fielding serving in the park store. Betty cooked hot scones and served them with jam and cream for the campers on wintry evenings. *LEE JONES*

*Left.* Lee Jones holding a groper that she caught at Kurnell. *Right.* Franz Borsova with part of his day's catch. *LEE JONES*

Enjoying camping in the Reserve during the 1950s. *Lee Jones*

Franz waves farewell to the idyllic days of camping on the Reserve. *Lee Jones*

1967, permissive occupancy and camping permits were rescinded and large picnics were banned.

Enjoying a game of cricket on the Reserve cricket pitch, 1930s. This was the same cricket pitch on which Prince George, heir to the British throne, and his brother Prince Albert enjoyed a game of cricket on in 1881. *HARRY MORGAN*

The shelter shed on the cricket pitch. *LEE JONES*

## Cricket

Cricket used to be an Australian community sport and the cricket pitch in the Reserve on which the two princes had played a match with the locals in 1881 was much used until the 1960s.

## National Parks and Wildlife Service

The Captain Cook Landing Place Reserve came under the provisions of the National Parks and Wildlife Service Act in 1967 when the park was proclaimed

The shelter shed stood until October 1998 when it collapsed and was not replaced. STAN HISKINS

'an historic site' and the Trusteeship was transferred from the Lands Department. Towra Point was combined with Endeavour Heights and the Landing Place Reserve to become the Botany Bay National Park. In 1988 Bare Island and La Perouse were included in the Botany Bay National Park which now frames the two headlands of the bay. Though the character of the landscape at the entrance to Botany Bay does now differ, it would not be unrecognisable to the 18th century British and French maritime explorers.

NPWS recognises the cultural and environmental assets of Kurnell Peninsula and is dedicated to its conservation, enhancement and management. Within its visionary goals, NPWS would like to manage the entire peninsula as a 'Biosphere Reserve' using the UNESCO guidelines for combining industry and conservation.

Gary Dunnett, the NPWS Manager for the Botany Bay Area, says that their vision for Botany Bay National Park is that 'Kurnell should be a symbolic meeting place of cultures and a place of natural significance, with a sense of ownership, for all Australians because:
- It is symbolic as the meeting place of diverse cultures and may be seen as the point of initiation of a multicultural nation.
- It is an important site for exploring issues involving reconciliation with indigenous Australians.
- It contains a landscape that supported Aboriginal people for thousands of years and includes the permanent freshwater stream that provided drinking water for the Aboriginal people and for both the *Endeavour* and the First Fleet.
- It contains plants that are directly descended from those collected by Joseph Banks and Daniel Solander in 1770.

- It retains rare vegetation and endangered ecological plant communities.
- It preserves the southern headland of Botany Bay and provides opportunities for nature based recreational pursuits such as whale watching, bush walking and surfing.
- It preserves the Towra Point with its heritage of unique terrestrial and aquatic habitats.

'The central theme of the Botany Bay National Park is that of "the meeting place of two cultures". Although there is a great deal of ambiguity in the views of the broader Aboriginal community about how to consider this site, the local Aboriginal communities are clear that it is a place with a role in the reconciliation process'.

Boardwalk amongst the mangroves behind the Shark's Leagues Club is used by the Field Studies Centre. This was the approximate site of Connell's logging canal into Woolooware Bay.

The NPWS Discovery Centre at Kurnell displays a 'Wetlands Reflections' exhibition, which focuses on Towra Point and the 'Eight Days that Changed the World' exhibition, focusing on Captain Cook, and it also houses the National Parks and Wildlife Service shop.

## Botany Bay Field Studies Centre

The NSW Department of Education and TAFE established Botany Bay Field Studies Centre as a regional advisory centre for the promotion of environmental education. Visiting pupils learn to understand interrelationships and interaction in the total environment. Teachers participate with their classes in planning environmental programs and field trips to wetland, woodland and heath communities. Both teachers and students acquire an understanding and awareness of the functioning of natural ecosystems typical of the area.

Within walking distance of the Field Study Centre are several tracks that highlight plant species collected by Banks and Solander in 1770 and others that pass historical monuments. The Centre's location lends itself to offering programs centred on Aboriginal and early European history and studies of seashore, wetland, heath and woodland environments. The Centre's studies include Towra Point Nature Reserve, Cronulla Beach and environs – explaining beach nourishment, stabilisation and sea wall features, and the freshwater wetlands between the dunes – where students can study a sand dune stabilisation project which has halted 100 years of degradation and human impact on the natural environment. Facilities include classroom, audio-visual presentations, exhibitions, a reference library, video camera, and art and craft equipment.

# 5 Unique Towra Point

## Creation of Towra Point

Towra Point, part of the Kurnell Peninsula, is located only 16 kilometres south of the Sydney CBD. Kurnell was an island one million years ago. The fresh water Cooks/Georges River System that emptied into Bate Bay separated it from the then mainland. When the sea level was stabilising, a tombolo (sand spit) was laid down over sedimentary deposits from the old rivers and linked Kurnell to Cronulla. Towra Point is the Holocene mud and sand delta that built up between the ancient Cooks and Georges Rivers before they changed their course some 10,000 years ago.

Aerial view of Towra Point. Kurnell Village and Caltex are in the background, sandmining can be seen to the right. *SUTHERLAND SHIRE ENVIRONMENT CENTRE*

As Towra Point was formed, sedimentary deposits from the ancient rivers covered the rich peat substrate. This produced a unique and delicate foundation for the establishment of the largest and most accessible extent of mangroves and saltmarsh areas in the Sydney region. About 50 per cent of the remaining

View from the end of the causeway looking into Towra wetlands, 2000.

mangroves and most of the saltmarshes within Sydney are to be found here in the Towra region of Botany Bay. Tidal currents, dredging and port works, together with waves from ocean swells and winds across Botany Bay and Woolooware Bay, today influence the shape of the 600 hectare Towra Point which has become a major breeding, feeding and roosting site for many threatened bird species.

Recognition of the threatened ecological biodiversity of Towra Point came in 1974 when Australia signed the International Convention for the protection of Wetlands of International Significance. In 1975, the Federal Government acquired 281.7 hectares of land at Towra for conservation as a nature reserve, which has since been extended to 410 hectares. It was the first Nature Reserve to be established by the Federal Government in Australia. When the Commonwealth/State Land Exchange Agreement was signed in 1979, Towra Point wetlands reserve was transferred from the Federal Government to the State Government.

Approximately 200 bird species have been recorded in the Towra Point Reserve. The flora is the last remnant of the type of vegetation that would have dominated the Botany Bay area. Nearly 300 plant species have been identified. The conservation significance of the wetland complex – with its diversity of habitats ranging from littoral forest, tidal wetlands, seagrasses, mangroves, saltmarshes, sandspits, bars, mudflats, dunes and beaches, occupying approximately 400 hectares – is recognised by Local, State and Federal governments. The fact that this primordial remnant endures within the Sydney area is extraordinary.

## Ownership of Towra Point

Many owners have held Towra Point since John Connell first purchased it in 1835. After the two John Connells came John Connell Laycock followed by Thomas Holt. Until the early 1960s Towra Point was home to a small number of oyster farmers and their families. Over later years it has been held in part by various firms including the Holt group of companies, L. J. Hooker, T. E. Breen (Consolidated Developments), Wendifyl Estates, Besmaw, Towra Point Developments, and Towra Construction.

*Left.* Looking through the littoral rainforest towards Botany Bay. *Right.* Erosion on Towra Beach. 1999. The rainforest used to extend a further 50 metres into the Bay from the present shoreline.

Towra Beach 1999, looking towards Port Botany and the city of Sydney. *DAPHNE SALT*

## International Conservation Agreements

The Wetlands of Towra, a rare ecosystem, are the only ones within the Sydney region accorded special protection under the Convention on Wetlands of International Importance, commonly referred to as the Ramsar Convention. The significance of Towra Point is so great that two other international agreements also recognise it, the Japan Australia Migratory Bird Agreement and the China Australia Migratory Bird Agreement. Preservation of the Towra Wetlands is critical to threatened bird, fish and shellfish species. The Wetlands are a vital link in the worldwide chain of habitats used by many migratory waders and shorebirds.

## Wetlands

Seagrasses. The waters around Towra Point support meadows of seagrasses. The main species are eelgrass *(Zostera),* strap weed *(Posidonia)* and paddle weed *(Halophila).* Preferring a soft sedimental bed like sand and mud, these flowering plants grow below the low tide level in the sheltered shallow waters.

Mangroves. The majority of mangroves are concentrated on the tidal margins of the bays. They excrete salt from their leaves and have the remarkable ability to change salt water into fresh. Mangroves produce significant amounts of leaf litter called 'detritus', which breaks down and provides food for aquatic plants and invertebrate animals. They help to reduce water pollution, provide shelter, refuge and food for many forms of marine life, prevent bank erosion and act as nurseries for fish species.

Saltmarshes. Saltmarshes are distinguished by an absence of trees and are dominated by herbs, grasses and low shrubs. A saltmarsh is only covered by high tide during 'king tides' (the highest of the spring tides) which occur three or four times a year. The vegetation is limited to rushes, succulents, sedges and a few other salt-tolerant plant communities growing in the waterlogged soils. Mangroves and saltmarshes co-exist.

Towra Dunes. These dunes were excavated in the mid 20th century, leaving man-made lakes as deep as 10 metres below sea level. It has taken more than two decades since the ending of the sandmining on Towra for the artificial lakes to evolve into fragile ecosystems which sustain a population of the endangered Green and Golden Bell Frog and migratory and wading birds.

Littoral Forest. Small groves of littoral rainforest in the Reserve support endangered plant species. In the rainforest areas the canopy is sometimes closed, above an understorey of ferns; but today the native seedlings are struggling to survive against the impact of an invasion by lantana. Introduced noxious weeds and feral animals also pose a threat to all flora and fauna in the Reserve. Fortunately the volunteer 'Friends of Towra' and parties organised by the

*Left.* The Great Wall of Towra during construction. *SSEC*

Sutherland Shire Environment Centre, with assistance of the National Parks and Wildlife Service, have regular working bees targeting these invaders and carrying out native bush regeneration.

Towra Lagoon. Captain Cook mapped Towra Lagoon in 1770 as a fresh water lake. Unfortunately, dredging in the once shallow Botany Bay has increased the

*Left:* The hemp bags rapidly deteriorated in the sun, allowing the wall to collapse under the impact of storms. Right: Salt water has again entered Towra Lagoon.

Looking into Towra Wetlands, 1999.

intensity of waves hitting Towra Point, threatening its overall ecology and causing the water in the lagoon to become extremely brackish so that its previous inhabitants such as the tortoise have disappeared. Some 40 metres of beach in front of the lagoon has been eroded. During 1997-98 environmentalist Bernie Clarke and the Environment Centre co-ordinated the construction of the 'Great Wall of Towra', a sandbag levee aimed at protecting Towra Lagoon from further inundation of salt water from Botany Bay. Unfortunately a big storm in May 1999 breached the wall.

## Gateway Proposal

NPWS is currently developing a proposal to construct a major environmental education facility at the entrance to the Kurnell Peninsula. The concept includes a floating boardwalk, a teaching, conference and interpretation centre, and an open-air theatre.

The proposal is in conjunction with Sutherland Shire Tourism Association and is centred on a former sandmining site that is now a constructed wetland. The facility will allow visitors to enjoy a wetland experience without disturbing the conservation values of the Nature Reserve.

## Horses

Horse stables are located near the entrance to Towra Point. The Nature Reserve is used as a venue for trail rides and by a riding school. Conservationists are strongly opposed to the presence of horses in this area, complaining that they

Kurnell Stables and Riding School adjacent to Towra Point, 1999.

spread weeds through their droppings and chop up sensitive surfaces with their hooves.

## Towra Point as an Airport?

It is not generally known that waterways on the southern shore of Botany Bay and at the entrance of Georges River came under private ownership in the nineteenth century. In the 1830s John Connell purchased Woolooware Bay for his logging interests. Then in 1864 Thomas Holt bought Gwawley Bay and Weeney Bay in the belief that a profitable oyster industry could be established. So these waterways were uniquely privateóa temptation to the owners to 'develop' them economically.

A century later, as the urbanisation of Sutherland Shire exploded, the Shire Council had to contend with this unusual phenomenon. Council actually agreed to acquire Holt's Gwawley Bay canals but found it had no funds. Eventually a private company developed the area as Sylvania Waters.

The Towra Point area, including Weeney Bay, remained privately owned. Since the 1880s it has changed hands many times, usually impelled by economic or access needs. But it still remains unoccupied and looks to most air travellers much the same as it did during the visits of Captain Cook and Governor Phillip.

Three years prior to the construction of the Caltex Oil Refinery in the early 1950s, Towra Point's flat wilderness was chosen by the Department of Civil Aviation as the natural place for Sydney's second international airport. In 1952 the Department of Civil Aviation built through it what it called a causeway to access a VAR Station (Visual Aural Radar) that it established to monitor the approach of aircraft to Mascot Airport. Meanwhile, the Department of Civil

Aerial view, 1999, of Towra Point and, in the background, Brighton. Captain Cook Bridge links Sans Souci and Brighton to Taren Point in Sutherland Shire. *DAPHNE SALT*

Aviation was involved in confidential discussions with the NSW State Planning Authority.

In a press release, 30 July 1965, the State Liberal MP for Cronulla, Mr Ian Griffith, praised the idea of an airport and pointed out that the Federal Department of Civil Aviation "desired to obtain approximately 1500 acres on the southern shore of Botany Bay bounded by Towra Point in the north to Wanda Recreation Reserve in the south, between Quibray Bay and Woolooware Bay…"

Intense protest from councils in the Sutherland Shire and St George area forced this scheme to be shelved. At the same time confidential discussions were being held with officers of Sutherland Council about the proposed airport, but were never disclosed.

The then Federal Member for Hughes, Les Johnson, raised the matter in question time in the Federal Parliament and the Hughes ALP Federal Council called a public meeting in the old Miranda Theatre on Sunday 8th October 1965 to protest the proposal.

The issue arose again, in 1967. A front page *Leader* article brought it to public attention (19.7.67). In a Presidential Minute to Council, 28th October 1968, Councillor Arthur Gietzelt advised the Council that the 'Outline Plan for the Sydney Region by the Minister for Local Government…. confirmed the fact that the establishment of a second airport at Towra Point was under consideration'.

Council unanimously opposed the proposal and asked State and Federal members for their support.

The largest-ever public meeting in Sutherland Shire up to that time, attended by five MPs and representatives of four neighbouring Councils and held in the parking area of Westfields Miranda, voted overwhelmingly against a Towra airport. The City press gave great publicity to the campaign and, then, to Prime Minister Gorton's decision to back off. Towra Point however remained as a large area with potential for development.

At the 1970 NSW Local Government Conference, Clr Gietzelt, on behalf of the St George and Sutherland Shire Councils, persuaded delegates to oppose any airport development on Towra. The conference agreed that Towra should remain a pristine and wetlands region.

In the 1970 Senate election Councillor Gietzelt was elected to the National Senate and continued his interest in retaining Towra Point as a protected area. Community forces also kept up the pressure.

Council was aware that the Commonwealth Department of Works was still working on plans for an airport in the area and it got wind that survey work was being done on about 390 acres owned by Wendifyl Estates Pty Ltd.

Shortly after election of the Whitlam Government in 1972, Senator Gietzelt raised the matter of the Federal Government acquiring Towra Point area as parkland; he was able to do so as a member of the Government's Urban Affairs Committee.

Prime Minister Whitlam acknowledged the need to acquire the area because of its unique closeness to Sydney (only 10 miles from the GPO), its wetlands character, and its overall value to the National Estate. Government Ministers Tom Uren and Moss Cass made similar representations, as did local members Ray Thorburn and Les Johnson. In 1974, Minister Cass finally won Cabinet approval. Money for its acquisition was provided in the second Whitlam Budget and discussions were opened with the NSW Liberal Government which had the power to acquire the land.

In May 1974 agreement was reached to acquire 1300 acres of Towra. Prime Minister Whitlam made a public statement at a press conference:

> People in this region are well aware of the impact on their environment of Kingsford-Smith Airport. They do not want another one. My Government has decided that there will be no expansion of Kingsford-Smith… We will build a second airport in Sydney but it will not be at Towra Point.
>
> Towra Point, as part of the Kurnell Peninsula, is a unique, natural wilderness area… indeed, the only one of its kind within 100 miles along the coastline of Sydney. Its preservation is essential to the ecology of Botany Bay. It has been under threat not only from an airport, but also from real estate developers.
>
> I therefore announce that the Australian Labor Government will acquire Towra Point and preserve it as a national park, so that it will become for all time a part of Australia's national heritage.

Tomorrow, May 8th, 1974, Australia will sign the International Convention for the Protection of Wetlands of International Significance. Towra Point is the last remaining wetland in greater Sydney and must be preserved.

So Towra Point, previously a privately owned area, remains a natural ecological gem in the greater Sydney Region. The residents of Sutherland Shire, especially in Sylvania Waters, Caringbah and Cronulla, have been spared to a major degree from excessive aircraft noise, and Sydney has saved the last major wetland area from development. It was a major victory for protecting the natural environment.

# 6 Early Enterprises

## Seaweed Harvest

The Second World War saw the drying up of gelatin imports from Japan. This was needed for the manufacture of agar – used in medical research, used as a thickening agent in products such as ice cream and tomato sauce, and used as the tenderiser and filler in tinned meats such as the army ration, Bullybeef. Extensive beds of the agar producing seaweed, *Gracialaria*, were discovered on the Kurnell side of Botany Bay. The seaweed was first crudely harvested by dragging an anchor through the weed beds. A little later a large rake about five to six feet long was dragged along the bed of the bay by a powerboat – tearing the plant up roots and all! Later still, a cutting blade shaped like a scythe was dragged behind the boats.

Seaweed harvesting anchor used in 1940. *DON CAMPBELL*

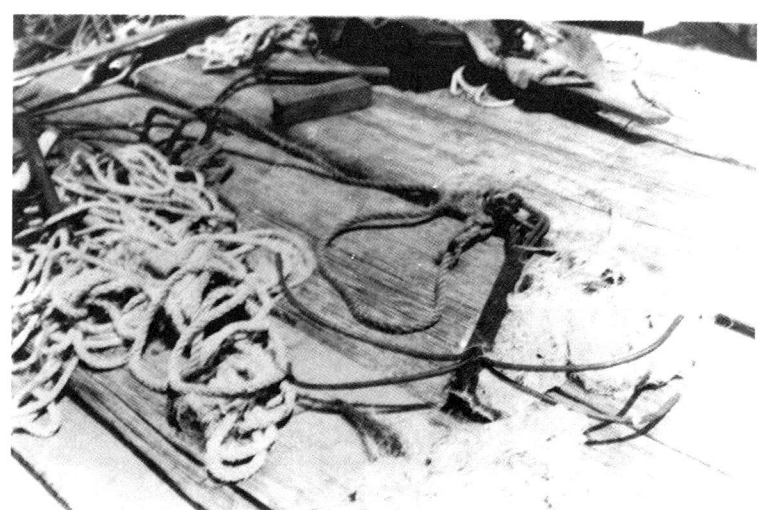

Because of their shape and shallow draft, 18-foot sailing hulls were used to bring the seaweed to the shore. *CHRIS HOLT*

Fred Bell's horses helped to bring the boxes of seaweed to the shore. *CHRIS HOLT*

The weed was also hung over fences and bushes, and indeed on any available surface. When wet, it was extremely heavy but after drying in the sun it was light enough to be handled in large volumes.

Alf Jacobs was hauling and turning the seaweed on Bonna Point the day the Second World War ended. He recalls: 'That was a funny day. Everybody was goin' to knock off work. I was the only bloke up the point there, turnin' over the seaweed. We 'ad all been told to knock off. I said, 'I'll just finish what I'm doin' 'ere, then I'll knock orf." I 'ad Buckley's chance.

'Jimmy Raine had a company and took the seaweed on Ray Pryor's truck to Cronulla then put it on a train and sent it off to Newcastle. 'E used to come out an' do all 'is deliverin' an' 'e'd pull up 'ere an' pick up a truck load of stuff to take back. The first truck was only a little two-wheeler one 'orse thing. But after

The seaweed took about a week to dry. It was spread on the grass at Bonna Point for that purpose. *CHRIS HOLT*

that 'e got a big one, a four-wheeler. It 'ad four 'orses. That was the one 'e used to come an' get the seaweed with.'

The seaweed was taken into the boatshed for sorting and baling, rather like wool or hay.

After the war, George Blundell carted the weed in his blitz wagon for Clarry Holt to Riverstone until storms and over-harvesting ended the enterprise. CHRIS HOLT

Each, every and any available surface, including vehicles, was used to dry the kelp. CHRIS HOLT

Blundell's blitz wagon loading weed from Fisher's Kurnell boatshed, 1949. *Chris Holt*

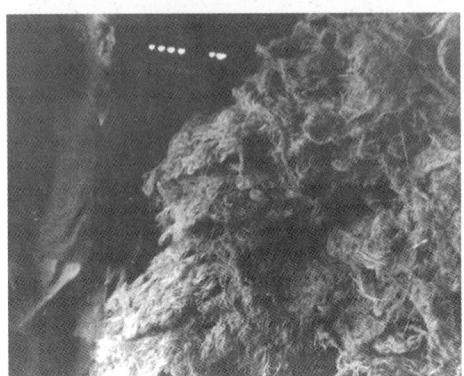

*Left.* The dry weed was carefully graded, sorted and loaded into a large press housed in the boatshed. *Right.* It was then compressed into 190-200 lb bales and bound with wire. *Chris Holt*

The bales, weighing 190-200 lb, were loaded onto the blitz wagon and transported through the dunes to Cronulla railway station, and thence by train to Sydney.

'We were getting about six pence a pound or nine pence a pound. By the time we'd dried it out you needed about 5000 lbs to make a quid.'

*Left.* Bale of seaweed. *Right.* The blitz wagon carried 8-9 tons of weed and was sometimes loaded up to 12 feet high. *Chris Holt*

Shells from the extinct Botany Bay mud oyster lie on the beach near Towra Lagoon, 1999.
*DAPHNE SALT*

## Early Oyster and Shell Gathering

Large native mud oysters, once prolific in Botany Bay, were relished by the Aborigines and were gathered by Captain Cook during his stay. Phillip also appreciated their abundance and it was to Botany Bay that he sent crews to gather them. They were sought not only for their delicious flavour but also for their shells. Divers were brought in from the Pacific islands to handpick the oysters. This resulted in massive over exploitation. So successful was the venture that by 1896 the then Fisheries Department declared mud oysters extinct. For more than a century none have been found in Botany Bay.

Despite the extinction of the mud oyster, an abundant supply of its shells remains in the Bay to this day. Shells were dredged from the seabed of Botany Bay

Looking south over the Cooks River Dam, 1870. A lime-burning kiln stands on the left. The dam had been built by a hundred convicts in 1840. The Cooks River now runs beside the Airport runways. It is a tributary of Botany Bay. *SUTHERLAND LIBRARY*

and transported to limekilns that were scattered around the waterways; there they were burnt and converted into lime for building.

## Shellgritters

Shellgrit gathering for the pet-bird and poultry industries began at the turn of the century. It had its heyday during the 1940s but was finished by 1956 when poultry farmers discovered that they could buy crushed oyster shells from the commercial oyster growers considerably cheaper than the old mud oyster shells dredged from the seabed of Botany Bay.

The crushed mud oyster shells were being sold at that time to the farmers for about 30 pence a 35lb sugar bag. The filled bags were taken to what is today the Water Police Wharf at Sans Souci and to Woolooware Bay where Lewis Anchorage is today. Apart from the local market, the grit was trucked to Parramatta and Gosford, with 150–250 bags to a truck depending on the size of the truck. There were many gritters involved in this lucrative business. Unfortunately three decades of intense dredging and raking of the seabed of Botany Bay irreversibly damaged large areas of the seagrass beds. Seagrasses and mangroves are maturing grounds for flathead, bream and other fish which lay their eggs at the headlands and rely on tides and currents to drift the spawn into the seagrass beds where the fish hatch and mature, relatively safe from predators. River garfish, which lay their eggs directly on the blades of the seagrass, are now gone from the Georges River because there is so little seagrass remaining for them.

## Boat Harbour Shellgrit

The beach at Boat Harbour, covered in densely packed small seashells, was an ideal shell-gathering region. 'Shellgrit' Charlie, one of the gatherers before World War II, shoveled crushed shell over his 'sieve', the wire mesh base of an old bed, then packed the graded grit into sugar bags before loading it onto his rubber-wheeled dray. Charlie also bought shellgrit from local lads who dug and bagged it for threepence a sugar bag. His laden dray was driven along the beach then to Cronulla railway station.

## Worms For Bait

Industrious oyster farmers and fishermen supplemented their income by supplying worms for bait to fishing-tackle shops. The worms were dug mainly in Quibray Bay, put into cardboard punnets lined with strands of seagrass, and sent all over the state.

One wormer in the 1950s was digging worms at the end of Kurnell's Bonna Beach when a new inspector came along and insisted on confiscating his shovel and worms. The wormer picked up his shovel, held it with both hands and said, 'You'll have to fight me for it!' The inspector replied, 'Well, I'm taking your worms.' The wormer retorted, 'Well, I'll give you the worms, where do you want 'em? In the car? Front seat or back seat?' 'In the back,' said the inspector. The wormer promptly opened the car door and tipped in the lot – water, sand, worms – all over the back seat! He commented later, 'I haven't been digging worms down there for a long while now!'

## The Oyster Industry

Fishing and oyster farming are the only pioneer industries surviving in the Shire today. The mud oyster was not the only oyster sought for the Sydney palate. The native estuary oyster that covers the tidal rocks and mangrove roots has an even more delicate flavour than the mud oyster. In 1811 a fisherman named Turpin added bags filled with Georges River and Weeney Bay estuary oysters to his catch when he sent it to market. By the 1830s oyster gatherers in the Georges River and various Kurnell bays provided the main supply to the Sydney market. Indiscriminate harvesting of both mud and estuary oysters prompted the Government to impose a total ban on harvesting all oysters for three years from 1870.

Farming the estuary oyster had its Australian birth with Thomas Holt's experiments. In 1856 he saw an advantage in cultivating rather than just harvesting oysters. While touring the Continent in 1863 he inspected the oyster culture industry in France and consulted world experts on the subject. When he returned to Australia in 1864 he bought Gwawley Bay for the sum of £80 and Weeney Bay for £100. He then procured the services of 200 convicts to customise his bays. Gwawley was to be the spawning area and Weeney the maturing area. They shored up the banks of Gwawley Bay with tree trunks and dug 300 claires (channels) totalling 30 miles in that bay. Then they erected a bridge across the mouth of the bay to Taren Point and put in floodgates to control the level of the water. The claires were filled with oysterlings (immature oysters)

Sandstone slabs laid down in the bays around Towra Point for a maturing oyster crop.

Oyster cultivation at Carters Island, using poles on forks of branches, 1922.

from Woolooware Bay, Georges River and Oyster Bay. But the venture proved an expensive failure. It fell victim to the turbidity (muddiness) of Gwawley Bay's water which, together with the excessive temperatures of the rock-hindered water in summertime and the predations of a red worm, served to destroy the unfortunate oysters.

At the expiration of the three-year ban, tenders were called for the lease of the whole of Botany Bay and its tributaries. Mr A. Emerson was the successful applicant. He re-sited undersized oysters to Weeney Bay for maturing. By 1920 there were 40,000 sandstone slabs at Towra and 450,000 at Pelican Point and Stinkpot Bay for the spats (oyster spawn) to cling to. In later years oyster farmers began to use logs, and later elevated wooden racks, to collect the drifting oyster spats.

Fred Sellman owned Bonna Point and Shell Point oyster leases until the 1950s when he handed his holdings over to the Council because he couldn't afford payment of the Council rates.

Bernie Clarke says that 1994 saw the outbreak of QX disease. QX is a marine haplosporidium virus, not to be confused with cryptosporidium, a fresh water virus. The Q is for its Queensland origin and X for unknown. It is thought that the trigger favourable to the virus, which caused the decline of much of Botany Bay's oyster industry, was acid sulphate. The 18 metre deep Holocene mud deposits, laid down in the ancient riverbeds beneath Botany Bay, had remained undisturbed for 10,000 years, but dredging and pumping up large quantities of this sedimentary mud to be used as land fill, exposed it to air, thereby oxidising it and converting it into acid sulphate – similar to the sulphuric acid used in a car batteries.

Thirty years ago some of the Bay's fish began to show red spots. It has now been established that Red Spot is directly linked to acid sulphate. So excessive levels have been present in Botany Bay for many years! Dredging began in the Georges River in the late 1950s, and the kelp/seaweed harvesting industry operated from the early 1930s through to the 1960s. Today 60 per cent of the Botany Bay-Georges River oyster industry is in the bays around Towra Point. Quibray Bay has the last mass stand of *Posidonia australis* seagrass, the deepwater seagrass that oxygenates the water. It is the only place where oysters can safely be set to depurate (purify).

## Fishing

The fish in Botany Bay were probably the staple diet of the Aboriginal people. A commercial fishing industry in Botany Bay commenced in 1790 operating mainly from the northern side, though there were isolated fishing shanties right around the bay from the earliest years. In 1815 James Birnie was granted his Alpha Farm and there he installed his caretaker/ manager who, apart from setting up the farm, fished the bay and sent the catch to Sydney along with his other produce.

The Booralee fishing village at Botany, on the northern shore of Botany Bay, was the first commercial fishing village in Australia. It began in the late 1820s and the name is an Aboriginal word meaning 'burley'. Today, the last three fishing dwellings in Booralee Street, though extensively renovated, have heritage classification. The relatively recent industrial and port complex of Botany now dwarfs them.

By the 1850s fishermen had built many shacks on the shores of Boat Harbour and Weeney, Woolooware and Quibray Bays, and sent their salted catch across the Bay to the Sydney market.

Bernie Clarke and two fishing mates, both stonemasons, had a shack on the hill at Boat Harbour in the 1930s. The stone masons built the best chimney in the whole of the Kurnell/Cronulla area. Bernie drove a Singer sedan and would let

Two of the last three cottages of the Booralee Street fishing village, Botany.

Bernie Clarke's fishing shack at Boat Harbour, 1936. *BERNIE CLARKE*

the tyres half down so that he could get through the bog spots. 'It was a hard place to get to.'

Though permissive occupancy at Boat Harbour has been rescinded, there are still about twenty fishing shacks there today.

During the second half of the nineteenth century there were at least seventy professional fishermen working Botany Bay and the Georges Rivers. As the relentless pursuit of seafood persisted, the numbers of fish diminished so that by 1920 there were less than 25 professional fishermen still operating in Botany Bay.

The remaining 20 fishing shacks at Boat Harbour in 1999.

Brian (Seaweed Morgan), Bob (Baldie) Morgan and Billy Dare at Boat Harbour hauling in their catch, 1960s. *HARRY MORGAN*

From the 1940s to the 1960s conditions improved and increasing numbers of professional handline and net fishermen plied the waters of Botany Bay and the ocean 'outside', often returning with catches of large fish. Huge mullet schooled into the bay and along Silver Beach towards Bonna Point. Astute fishermen watched for their rising near Alpha House and set their nets from the beach at Bonna Point. They were often rewarded with impressive hauls. Sometimes they even joined three nets together to hold a bumper catch.

The wharf in the Reserve near the Cook Obelisk, built in 1902 by the Lands Department, was a popular fishing spot for the locals and the visitors. But it was

Sorting and loading the morning's catch at Boat Harbour, 1960s. *HARRY MORGAN*

Blissenden's fishing shack at Boat Harbour, 1986. *LEE JONES*

inconvenient for the professional fishermen; so they constructed a wharf off the end of Dampier Street. Unfortunately the tide was out when D. T. Match crossed the bay by ferry for the opening ceremony and the ferry was unable to approach the Dampier Street wharf. The ferry took him to the park wharf instead and he

Harry Morgan snr, Len Elie, Cess Kemp and young Harry Morgan landing their catch in the 1960s. *HARRY MORGAN*

The Dampier Street wharf, also known as 'Shag's Rest', with fish traps on its deck. *George Blundell*

was obliged to return to Dampier Street wharf by pony cart to officiate. The Dampier Street wharf earned the name of 'Shag's Rest' and was strictly a high tide access wharf. Eventually it fell into disrepair, its remains being reported locally to be good firewood.

Several of the professional fishermen of 50 years ago had served their time as boat builders. In slow fishing periods they were able to turn their hand to their craft. The Fisher family, who owned and ran the ferries, built them at La Perouse. They also towed a boatshed from Sydney Harbour on a punt and re-erected it adjacent to Silver Beach Road in the 1920s. Bill Fisher built skiffs in this shed that has withstood all storms. It has been used for a sailing club, for seaweed harvesting and for boat building. Peter Bracken rented it and built his boats there before moving into his own shed in Ward Street. Today it is owned by Pete McWilliams, a retired professional fisherman who bought it from Bill Fisher in 1960 and continues to build boats there.

The recreational fishermen formed a fishing club that had its headquarters at Bonna Point. John Jones recalls that, in the 1950s, 'Down the waterfront there at one time you'd get flounder over a foot long and ten inches wide and flathead up to three feet long – with a broom-stick and a six inch nail and just stab 'em! Lobsters, Gawd strike me, you'd go up on the boulders there opposite the flagstaff and you could bend over and pick 'em up, lobsters over a foot long. It was nothing to pick up about 50 or 60 lobsters.'

Despite all the dredging, plus the development of the oil refinery and the construction of the airport runways, commercial fishing and prawn trawling remains active in Botany Bay and recreational fisherman too, can sometimes carry home a respectable catch.

The boatshed on Silver Beach was brought to Kurnell from Sydney Harbour by a tug towing it on a barge, 1999. *DAPHNE SALT*

In January 2000, NSW Premier Bob Carr announced a plan to introduce a $25 a year recreational fishing license along the coast to help fund a compulsory buy-out of the 90 commercial fishing licenses operating in Botany Bay and its tributaries and use the funds for fish-breeding programs. Botany Bay is one of NSW's most important fish nursery habitats and stocks are severely depleted. This announcement was met with protest by both commercial and recreational

Net fishermen hauling in their catch in 1999 on Silver Beach between the groynes. Pelicans and other seabirds wait for their handout. The oil refinery wharf can be seen in front of the Reserve.

fishermen. However, as one fisherman stated: '…the problem is really with the state of the river itself, which still isn't being addressed.'

## Fish Farm

Australia's first, and eastern Australia's only, marine fin fish farm, the four hectare 'Silver Beach Aquaculture', is situated today close to the southern side of the Caltex wharf in Botany Bay. The Department of Fisheries established this experimental fish farm; its trialling was taken over by John Hedison in 1996. In the submarine pens there are thousands of snapper and jewfish, destined for Sydney restaurants. The fish farm is a futuristic project and a unique farming venture that requires John to work seven days a week, for six to eight hours a day, feeding the fish, doing repairs and changing the nets. He is experimenting with alternative feeding methods for his aquaculture, to minimise impact on the environment. Scallops, pearl oysters and mussels are to be installed around the site to take up additional nutrients released into the water from feeding of the fish.

Fish hatcheries on the mid north coast of NSW grow fingerlings from spawn to stock the bays and estuaries. They also supply fingerlings to John, who says he prefers to concentrate on the jewfish because they grow faster and are not susceptible to parasites. After 18 months they reach about 2 kg and are 60cm in length; being a uniform clean colour they are highly prized by gourmets, and especially by overseas tourists.

John Hedison's fish farm near the Caltex wharf at Kurnell supplies snapper and jewfish to Sydney restaurants, 1999.

Aquaculture off Kurnell's Silver Beach

## Ducks

Many Kurnell people kept ducks, some for their own table and some for the city market. Mr Ducksbury (his actual name) had a small duck farm between Prince Charles Parade and Torres Street. There was also an establishment known as Taylor's Duck Farm, at the back of Marton Hall, off the end of Bridges Street, where the equestrian centre is located now. Mr Taylor, who kept bulldogs to guard the property also ran a seed business. Taylor's farm extended over to the south side of Solander Street. The ducks were raised for their eggs, their feathers for pillows and their delicate meat. The droppings were sold as fertiliser. George Blundell, owner of a series of ex-army blitz wagons, operated as a carrier and carted large crates of ducks to the markets, returning with feed and other produce.

After the Duck Farm closed, the site was planted with mulberry trees and a silkworm farm sprang up there. It lasted until the 1970s, and was followed by a butterfly farm. It is now an equestrian centre. *HARRY MORGAN*

## Chooks

No Australian can call a chicken anything but a chook and many backyards had their chooks. Kurnell was no exception. Mrs Ingle, who had the honour of installing Kurnell's first windmill, had a poultry farm. So did the Honnor family, who kept a hundred chooks as well as running a shop, holiday houses and an apiary of several hundred hives. The honey was sold to Norco. John Graham Weir, who ran 400 chooks, was years ahead of his time with his organic garden, fertilised with seaweed in the backyard of his home which stretched between

Torres Street and Prince Charles Parade. The Egg Board who bought his eggs regulated the poultry quota. Foxes were prevalent in the district and could wipe out scores of chooks in one night if they gained entry to a yard. Kurnell was still a 'farmy' place when the rest of the Sydney suburbs were being absorbed into a highly urbanised metropolis.

Caroline Weir (Davis) feeding the chooks on her father's poultry farm, 1947. *CAROLINE DAVIS*

## Wild Sheep and Pit Ponies

Thomas Holt had put sheep on his Kurnell land in 1868, a venture that ended in disaster, as described earlier. Surviving sheep were left to roam and became feral. In the 1930s there were still a few of them in the wilds of the headland and heath. They grew to a larger size than the normal farm animals, resembling wild goats rather than sheep according to an old resident who saw them as a child.

When coal mines at nearby Helensburgh and Wollongong needed pit ponies, John LeHane, one of the Shire's first councillors, devoted one of his farms at Caringbah to raising them. Apart from growing lucerne on the 'Highfields' (Caringbah) and grazing his cattle on agistment in the Captain Cook Landing Place Reserve, he capitalised on the need for the pit ponies, allowing them to roam throughout Kurnell feeding on its then plentiful fodder. The handwritten Reserve Trust records reveal that in March 1909 Thomas LeHane paid £25/2/9 (approx. $50) per quarter for his lease of grazing rights on the reserve. When the mines were mechanised there was no further need for these hardy horses. They were left on the peninsula to fend for themselves.

Roaming sheep, cattle and horses were prevented from wandering to Cronulla by a fence and gate located approximately where the Cronulla High School is today.

## Dairies

Many of the village people had their own cows but there were also several dairies. Ted Whiteman's dairy was on Dampier Street and Bob Bland had another on the site of today's Abbotts Laboratories.

Stillwells Dairy was on the eastern side of Cook Street, on the higher ground above the swamp, and it extended into the oak forest near the eastern end of Solander Street – now part of the Caltex Oil Refinery site.

Cattle from one of the dairies, grazing by a swamp, 1953. *SUTHERLAND LIBRARY*

# 7 Industries Intrude

## The Noxious Reserve

As a result of the 1848 Act of Parliament banning noxious industries from Sydney proper, these industries were attracted to the areas around Botany Bay with its plentiful water supply. The Noxious Traders Association was formed in the 1870s to control malodorous and polluting activities such as power plants, tanneries, glue works, soap works, wool-scouring mills, lime burning kilns and sewage farms. In 1883, a Royal Commission suggested Kurnell Peninsula as the site for Sydney's noxious trades because of the threat of bubonic plague and the 'disgustingly offensive' odors in the air. The likelihood of such a siting increased when the Como Railway Bridge was opened in 1886 and the railway was extended to Sutherland. That same year, Parliament passed a bill to resume and dedicate 3570 acres of land at Kurnell for noxious trades, waste and a cemetery; and a branch railway line was proposed to link it to the main line at Sutherland.

Cemeteries were then classified as toxic regions because the runoff from the leachate in the soil after rains was believed to cause health problems. Nineteenth century maps show a proposed mortuary railway from Sutherland to the Noxious Reserve at Kurnell. However the opening of Woronora Cemetery on Linden Street in Sutherland in 1893 put an end to that plan. But the noxious trades and waste classification still applied to Kurnell Peninsula.

## Alterations of Botany Bay

The year that Birnie obtained his Kurnell grant, 1815, Simeon Lord built a textile mill, followed ten years later by a flour mill, on the Lachlan Stream (now known as the Mill Ponds), on the northern side of Botany Bay adjacent to the now airport. There were three other wool-scouring mills on the northern side of Botany Bay by 1885. The Sydney City Sewage Farm was built in 1890 at the entrance to Cooks River, almost next door to the Lachlan Swamps at Botany (the Lachlan Swamps supplied Sydney with water for sixty years). Public pressure arising again from the threat of diseases such as the bubonic plague prompted the formation of the Sydney Harbour Trust in 1901 to control all of Sydney's waterways. Sixty years later it became the Maritime Services Board. The sewage farm closed in 1916.

The Banksmeadow Long Pier, also on the northern side of Botany Bay, was built for colliers from the Hunter River in 1880. In 1921 the Commonwealth Government acquired 64.5 hectares of land beside Cooks River for the development of an airport, though it was not until after the Second World War that major airport work began.

The mouth of Cook's River was moved 1.25km south, the mangroves were cleared and the wetlands reclaimed.

In 1953 the Australian Oil Refinery was established at Kurnell and a jetty of more than a kilometre in length was constructed to provide a berth for tankers.

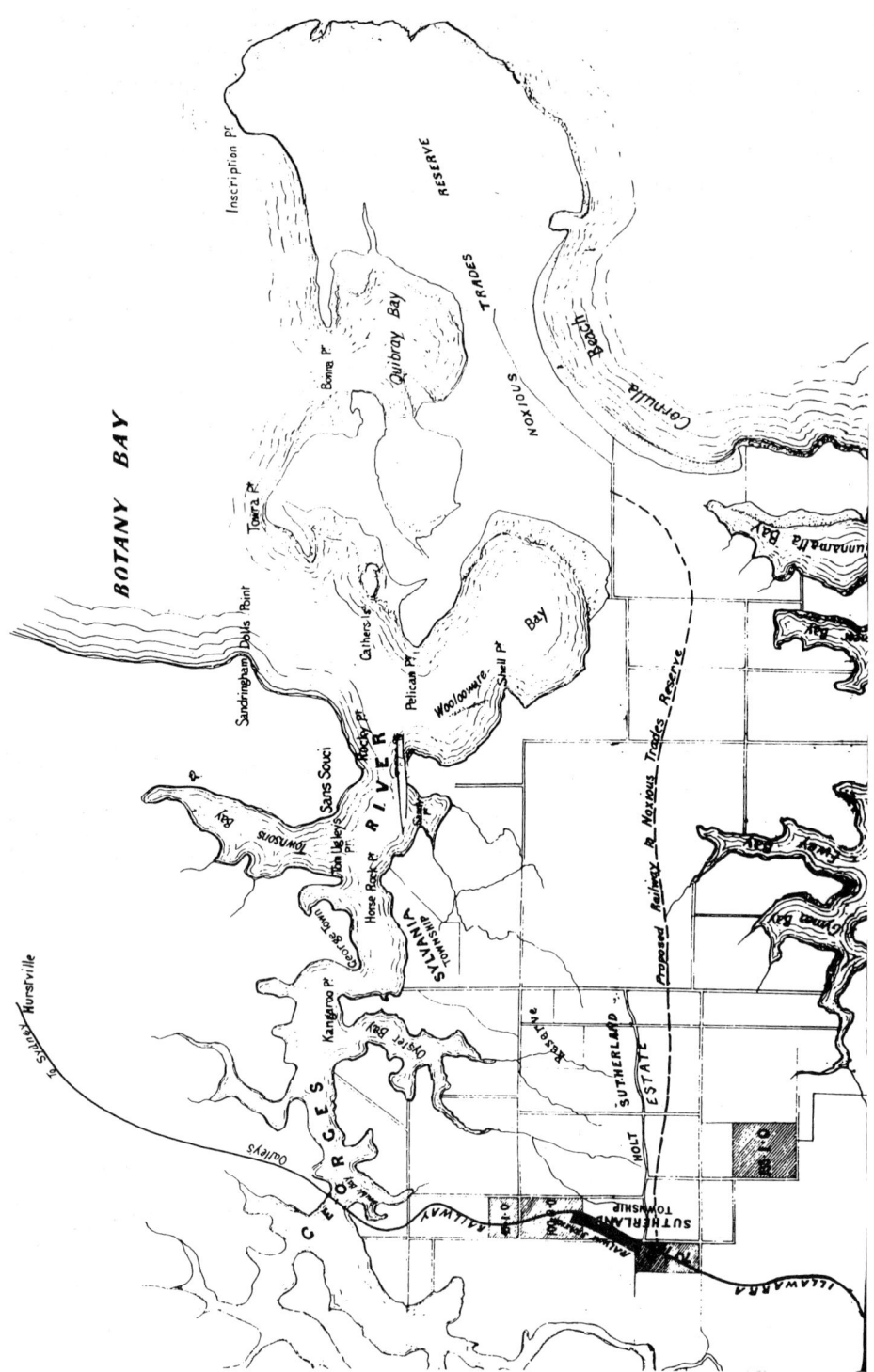

Map showing proposed railway link from Sutherland to Kurnell Noxious Trades Reserve, 1886.
SUTHERLAND LIBRARY

During the 1960s, the Maritime Services Board assumed responsibility for Port Botany. In 1962 a research program headed by English experts, recommended to the NSW Government that a new port to handle the super-tankers be built on the northern side of Botany Bay.

The size, power and numbers of aircraft increased and work began to build airport runways into Botany Bay. Over the next twenty years these runways were extended and Port Botany container terminal and Banksmeadow chemical storage facility were developed. Extensive dredging to overcome the problem of the shallowness of Botany Bay and to provide mooring facilities for large ships and for the airport runways was undertaken. A V-shaped channel two km long and 21.3 metres deep was dredged. The dredged material was used to reclaim 600

The Belgian bucket dredge Goomoi, working in Botany Bay, 1960s. *GEORGE BLUNDELL*

The dredge discharging its load of sand onto the first airport runway, 1966. *GEORGE BLUNDELL*

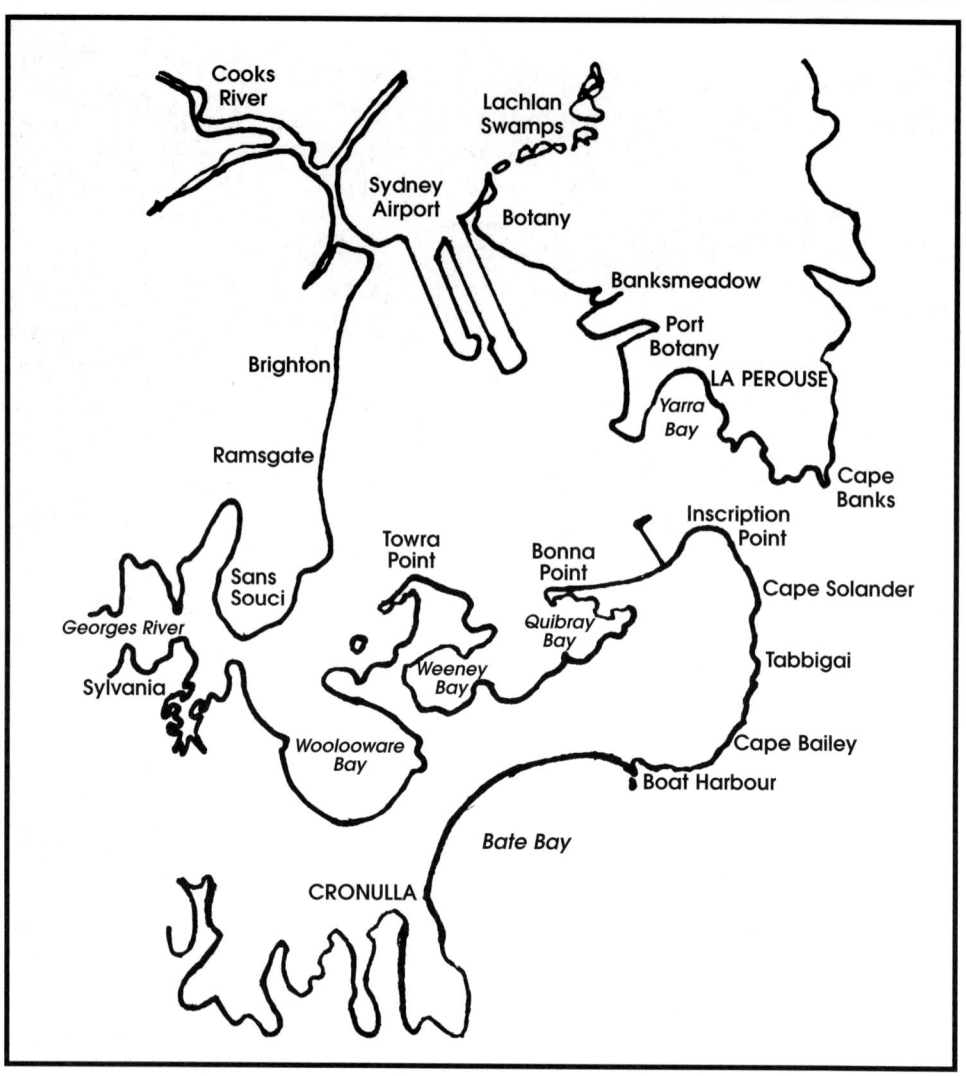

Location map of the Botany Bay region.

hectares of land from the bay and foreshores for the new port, for the runways and for industrial development.

The shoreline of Botany Bay has been increased by nearly 20 per cent by adding extra runway and port structures to the original shoreline, but the resultant impact on the ecosystem has been devastating. Dredging the bay has significantly altered wave direction, causing ongoing severe erosion along the western (Brighton) shore of the Bay and along the southern shore of Kurnell Peninsula. Protective groynes were built to absorb the altered, and now more powerful, wave energy impacting on Lady Robinsons Beach to the west and Kurnell's Silver Beach to the south. They have reduced but not stopped the erosion, and more than 50 per cent of the natural Botany Bay shoreline has had to be reconstructed.

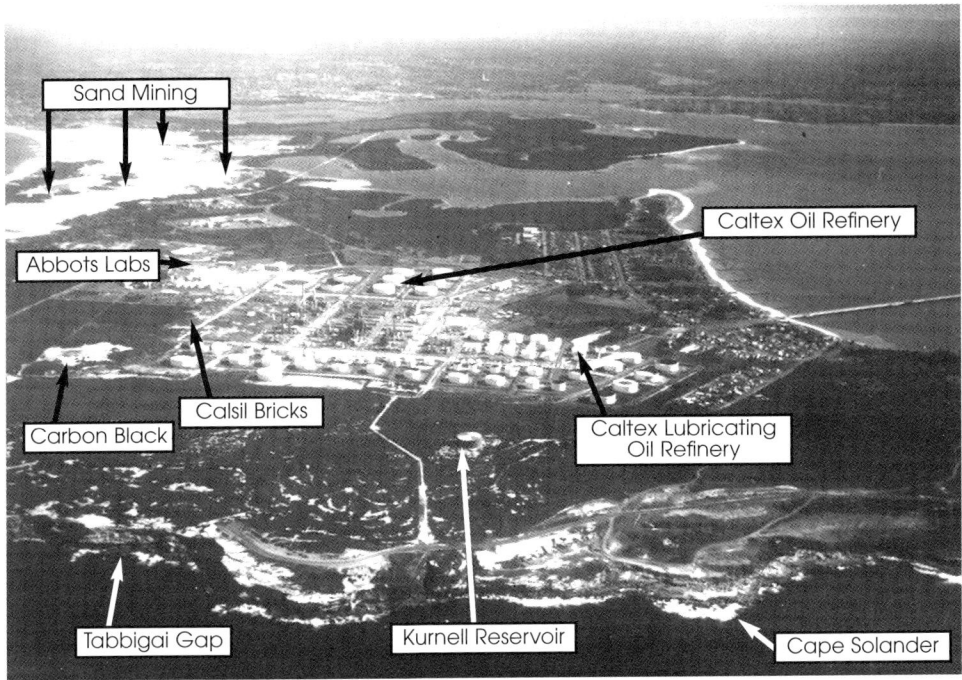

Sand Mining

Caltex Oil Refinery

Abbots Labs

Calsil Bricks

Carbon Black

Caltex Lubricating
Oil Refinery

Tabbigai Gap

Kurnell Reservoir

Cape Solander

Aerial view of Kurnell showing some of the industry.

Aerial view of Caltex, Calsil/ Boral Bricks and Continental Carbon industrial plants, 1999.

Continental Carbon

Sand was taken from
Crown Land to replenish
Silver Beach in 1974

Caltex Oil Refinery

Boral/Calsil Bricks

The Continental Carbon Company during construction. This series of six photographs was taken from a nearby sand dune in the 1950s. *LEE JONES*

Kurnell could very rightly be called the Black and White Peninsula – the white for its sandmining and its sand-made Calsil bricks, the black for its oil refineries and carbon black plants.

Industry has imposed a heavy footprint on the once pristine landscape of Kurnell. One century after it was designated for noxious trades and waste, the Kurnell Peninsula has largely become an industrial wilderness.

## Private Ownership on the Peninsula

Of the 875 hectares of land on the peninsula, some 55 per cent is in private ownership. Apart from the residential occupation of the land, Caltex Oil Refinery is by far the largest industrial establishment. In 1966 two carbon black manufacturing factories were established near the refinery on permanent leases of Crown Land. Abbotts Laboratories was built in 1962 on eight hectares of its 70-hectare holding to manufacture a range of chemicals and pharmaceuticals. Calsil Bricks, now operated by Boral, has a perpetual lease of two hectares on Sir Joseph Banks Drive where it makes concrete bricks. The 35 hectares owned by Imperial Chemical Industries is vacant land from which sand is being extracted.

The Holt family, by 1861 the owner of almost the entire Kurnell Peninsula, has since sold much land but still retains an enormous amount. The Holt group of companies is the largest of the sandmining ventures. Breen Holdings, a large Kurnell sandmining concern since the 1950s, also continues sandmining operations while controlling the Kurnell Landfill, a tip for non-putrescible waste materials. Among the other large landholders on the peninsula are Consolidated Developments and urban developer, Australand. The Sutherland Shire Council and Sydney Water also own parcels of land.

In 1986, a German chemical giant, Bayer, lodged a development application to establish a plant at Kurnell for the formulation and packaging of chemical products. The proposal was highly controversial and attracted shire-wide community opposition. A Commission of Inquiry and an Environmental Impact Study were undertaken. Bayer had invested a large amount of money in purchasing the site, and it invested more in fighting its case in the Inquiry and against the community campaign. The stringent conditions and controls required by the Commission to protect the surrounding ecosystem were finally announced by Bayer to be so onerous that it felt compelled to abandon the project as uneconomic. The outcome was hailed as an environmental victory for the people of Kurnell, the wider Sutherland Shire community and Sutherland Shire Council.

Within Kurnell Village itself there are 25 to 30 smaller industrial establishments ranging from steel-fabricating and automotive repair works to electrical engineering, refrigeration, plastics and concrete products manufacture.

Lakes, secondary to sandmining, have here replaced the dunes, 1999.

## Sand Mining

The effects of 'development' are still being worked out as considerable sand extraction continues on the peninsula. The sand has been long valued by the building industry because of its high crushed shell content and lack of organic matter. The sand dunes of Kurnell have provided a cheap source of sand for much of Sydney, but as a result of this exploitation Kurnell has been robbed of its original character. Removal of the sand has significantly weakened the peninsula's capacity to resist storms. Ocean waves pounding the reduced Kurnell dune system have threatened to break through to Botany Bay, especially during the storms of May–June 1974 and August 1998.

Sand from the dunes on the throat of Kurnell headland has been extracted since the 1930s when the State Government granted mining leases on freehold and Crown Land. In April 1937, Haymarket Land and Building Co. offered Sutherland Shire Council 720 acres of land at the entrance to Kurnell for £8 per acre. Many of the councillors wished to create a National Park at Kurnell, 'the

Aerial view of the sand dunefields in the 1920s shows that dunes are still largely covered by vegetation (right middleground). Boat Harbour is in the left foreground and Quibray Bay and Botany Bay in the background. *SUTHERLAND LIBRARY*

Birthplace of Australian History and Gateway to Captain Cook's Landing Place', and to include in it the dunes and Towra Point. The Council was evenly split, but C. O.J. (Joe) Monro, the Council's President [today termed Mayor], argued that

Aerial view, 1998, showing deep ponds where sand dunes formerly towered up to 200 feet. *ANNETTE HOGAN*

because the land 'was all sandhills it was completely useless'. He cast his deciding vote against the purchase. The sandhills were doomed from that point.

Sand deposits are still being worked, in 1999, by three privately owned companies:

1. Metropolitan Sand Company and Processed Sand Pty Ltd, both part of the group controlled by T. E. Breen. In 1952, a builder asked Breen, who was working as a reporter, where he could get large quantities of dry sand. This simple enquiry triggered Breen to research all aspects of sand usage and mining. The Breen sand extraction companies commenced mining in 1953.

Formerly the site of the towering sand dunes, now lakes and valleys, leaving only a few of the foredunes as protection against breakthrough by the sea, 1999.

2. Pioneer Concrete (NSW) Pty Ltd, under lease from Besmaw Pty Ltd, one of the Holt group of companies. The Holt family has owned Kurnell land since 1861, and sand mining on their land began as Allsands in 1953.

3. Hooker Industrial Sands, now Metromix, mined sand since 1967 on land leased from Australian Consolidated Developments, another of the Holt group.

Sand has also been extracted periodically from Crown Lands by both the local council and the state government. Crown Land adjoining Sir Joseph Banks Drive, notified as a Public Recreation Reserve in 1949, had this notification revoked in 1965. It was then designated a Reserve for Future Public

Potter Point, with its five unsightly vents, is where Sydney Water's Sewage Treatment Plant discharges effluent into the ocean, creating a health risk for nearby swimmers. This photograph looks south from the point across Boat Harbour to Cronulla beaches, 1999.

Requirements in expectation of sand extraction and industrial development ceasing. However, as the twentieth century draws to a close, the sandminers, finding their resources dwindling, are looking to further profit from the stripped land by building residential housing or recreational resorts or industrial complexes.

## Sewage Treatment Plant

Sydney Water owns the sewage treatment works on Captain Cook Drive. Treated effluent is discharged at an ocean outfall on Potter Point just north of Boat Harbour. The Sewage Treatment Plant is currently (1999) being upgraded and expanded.

## Caltex Oil Refinery

Oil refining had been carried out in Australia during the 1920s and 1930s, but until Caltex decided to refine crude oil near Sydney the industry had been small. In 1951 Caltex Oil Company approached the Sutherland Shire Council with a proposition to establish a major oil refinery at Kurnell. Caltex assured Council that 'there would be no smoke or nuisance of any kind'. The outcry from sections of the public was immediate. Initially Council refused consent on the grounds of 'consecration of the landing place of Captain Cook' and the impact on the community of such an industry. In 1952 this objection was conditionally withdrawn after the State Government granted approval to Caltex. The Government then instructed the Cumberland County Council (the body then

Vegetated dunes on the site of Caltex Refinery prior to commencement of construction, 1950. *George Blundell*

Clearing for the construction of Caltex Oil Refinery. *George Blundell*

responsible for subdivisions in Sydney) to suspend its existing zoning and draw up a plan for the future development of the Kurnell Peninsula. Caltex then purchased 174 hectares of land for the refinery site, but before building could commence an adequate heavy transport road had to be built. The only access to Kurnell at that time was a sandy track, maintained by Kurnell residents and the Latta Bus Company. The track, which traversed the sandhills and skirted Botany Bay, was partly inundated during 'king tides'.

Caltex (Standard Oil of California and Texas Co.) established a new subsidiary company known as Australian Oil Refining Pty Ltd (AOR). Following

Constructing a canal opposite the present service station, to drain water from the swamp on from the Caltex site. GEORGE BLUNDELL

an Act of Parliament approving the refinery and the site, construction began in December 1953.

By February 1956, AOR was pumping refined products by submarine pipes to the Banksmeadow Oil Terminal on the northern foreshores of Botany Bay. A Dutch dredging company and a team of men were brought to Kurnell for the construction of the pipelines across the bed of Botany Bay. They brought with

Sinking bores to test the sub-strata prior to the construction of the Caltex Refinery. GEORGE BLUNDELL

The Dutch-operated Belgian dredge nicknamed '2-11', excavating the bed of the Bay to facilitate construction of the bulk liquid wharf for Caltex. *GEORGE BLUNDELL*

Dutch migrants were employed for the construction of the wharf and the pipelines beneath Botany Bay, 1954. *SUTHERLAND LIBRARY*

them a Belgian dredge, towed by a tugboat, reportedly the largest dredge in the world at the time. The pipelines were laid while the refinery was being built.

Caltex built a residential hostel near Bonna Point, Kurnell, for the Dutch workers, many of whose wives and children came with them. Following the completion of the wharf and the pipelines, the Dutch company moved on to another project but many of the workers and their families had fallen in love with

A large pipe, part of the refinery's cracking plant, being transported on a low-loader along Polo Street, now Captain Cook Drive, to the refinery. Both ends of this pipe had been sealed in order to float and tow it from Sydney by tug. *GEORGE BLUNDELL*

Construction of the Caltex Oil Refinery, 1954. *SUTHERLAND LIBRARY*

the area and opted to settle permanently in Kurnell Village or elsewhere in the Sutherland Shire. A significant Dutch community remains here today.

During the peak construction period, 3000 men worked at the various sites. They were engaged in draining swamps, clearing scrub, providing water and

The pipes for AOR were trucked to Taren Point then brought to Kurnell by tug. *Left.* The pipe being lowered into the water where the lengths were coupled together by divers. *Right.* Diver Billy Gray goes down to join the pipes. *George Blundell*

sewerage facilities, and building the Caltex complex itself. This was the largest petroleum installation built in New South Wales by private enterprise. It included 56 storage tanks. Further expansion took place in 1964; a processing plant to refine Bass Strait crude oil was completed in 1973; and continuing expansion occurs as need arises.

The Refinery's wharf, more than a kilometre long, was completed in 1956 and upgraded in 1994. It is capable of berthing ships that have a cargo capacity of 60,000 dead weight tonnes. On the northern side of the wharf, pipelines connect the refinery's tanks to three shipping berths. The refinery produces

Aerial view of Caltex Oil Refinery, the wharf, Kurnell Village and Sivler Beach, 1978. *Caltex*

Towra Point

transport fuels. Pipes under Botany Bay are connected to BP, Mobil and Shell terminals at Banksmeadow and Silverwater, and to Mascot Airport.

The wharf has four remote-controlled fire monitors, three converted icebreaker ships on firewater standby, and simultaneous underdeck and fire hydrant systems in addition to emergency shut-off valves. The wharf also supports a cooling water pumphouse that provides the refinery's cooling water.

Adjacent to the AOR refinery is the Caltex Lubricating Oil Refinery (CLOR). Preparatory work began on the Crown Land at Kurnell in June 1961. CLOR commenced production in 1963 as Australian Lubricating Oil Refinery (50% Caltex, 25% Golden Fleece and 25% Ampol) and is now owned by Caltex. This refinery produces special grades of lubricant oil-based stocks, greases, naphthenic products (ink oils, heat treatment), waxes (waterproofing, building products, cosmetics).

Caltex is careful to cultivate a 'good neighbour' relation with Kurnell and Sutherland Shire. It sponsors many Kurnell activities including the Precinct and Progress Association's annual festival. It also gives assistance to community groups such as the Kurnell Sports and Recreation Club, Cronulla Red Cross, Police Citizens Boys Club, Guides and Scouts, Cronulla Leagues Club and Volunteer Bush Fire Brigade.

Kurnell Village is overshadowed by the refinery, 1999.

# $8$ Access and Services

## Ferries and Wharves

Ferries ran regular services from Sans Souci, on the eastern side of Botany Bay, and from La Perouse, at the north head of the Bay, as far back as 1898. After the construction of Captain Cook Drive, a macadamised road from Cronulla–Woolooware to Kurnell Village and the Refinery, passenger numbers fell and these services were running only intermittently by 1957. The last of the ferries ceased running in May 1965. There are currently plans for resuming the service from Brighton to Kurnell. The Brighton wharf is being modified to facilitate the service, though where it will berth at Kurnell is not yet clear.

The first wharf on record was the Holt wharf that extended from below the Cook obelisk out over what is known as Cook's Rock, where the Isaac Smith Memorial Tablet is affixed.

In 1899 the State Government resumed the land for the Captain Cook Landing Place Reserve and appointed the Lands Department as Trustee. The Department rebuilt nearby Alpha House and constructed a new wharf to serve employees of the Reserve, residents, fishermen and visitors. After the wharf was built the Fisher family, who operated a boatshed and ferry service at La Perouse, increased the number of their ferry services to Kurnell.

Thomas Holt's wharf built in the 1880s, showing the hoist and floating landing pontoon. An iron fence (later removed) still surrounds the obelisk in this photograph. This was the wharf used by recreational and professional fishermen and by the ferries until 1902. *MITCHELL LIBRARY*

The park wharf was maintained and kept in good condition, but was demolished by the storms of 1974. Until the 1960s it had the shelter-shed, 'the church', at the end of it. This was the wharf used during the 1970 royal visit for the Cook bicentennial celebrations.

The Lands Department built a new wharf about 100 metres to the north of the obelisk after demolishing the decayed Holt wharf in 1902. *Mitchell Library*

The shelter shed, occasionally called the 'church', on the park wharf. The church got its name from a fisherman who often spent his entire weekend on the wharf. The priest, coming over by ferry to take the service in the Roman Catholic Church, commented that he had not seen him at Mass for some time. The fisherman replied that he had been in the 'church' on Sunday. *Harry Morgan*

Park wharf decorated for the Cook landing celebrations 1950. The shelter shed can be seen on the wharf. *HARRY MORGAN*

Queen Elizabeth walking from the park wharf to the obelisk, April 1970. The royal yacht *Britannia* is in the background. *GEORGE BLUNDELL*

There was a second wharf, and perhaps a third, at Kurnell before the 1952 refinery wharf was built. The one most remembered was the Dampier Street wharf – because it was something of a failure! It was built with the intention of landing ferry passengers and also to allow the fishermen an easier access to their boats by avoiding a long walk up to the park. But it was strictly a high tide wharf.

Looking landward along the Dampier Street wharf in the 1940s. It was better known as the 'Shag's Rest'. *BETTY JACOBS*

At low tide there was no water within metres of it and it fell into disuse and decay.

Over the years the Fisher family had a string of ferries which they built at their La Perouse headquarters. Three of their other ferries, all 'steam boats', were the *Solander* which operated on the Hacking River, the *James Cook* which

Remains of the Dampier Street Wharf. Also, the railway sleeper retaining wall constructed in 1936 in an attempt to control erosion of the foreshores. *BETTY JACOBS*

The ferry *Cape Banks* leaving Kurnell. *ELSIE POPPLEWELL (HONNOR)*

operated in Sydney Harbour, and the *Erina* which operated in Botany Bay and also from the Cronulla Ocean Wharf to Sydney via Kurnell and La Perouse.

The *CAM Fisher* ferry approaching the central landing platform of the park wharf, 1920. The rocks in the foreground are adjacent to the Cook obelisk. *ELSIE POPPLEWELL*

*CAM Fisher* off Alpha House. This ferry after termination of the service in 1957 went to Victoria for a re-fit and has returned to the Georges River as the *Eucumbene* a touring function vessel.
ELSIE POPPLEWELL

## Vexed Issue – a Road from Cronulla to Kurnell

Access to Kurnell was a vexed issue for many decades, beginning even before the formation of the Sutherland Shire Council in 1906. From the start, the Council agreed on the need for a road from Cronulla to Kurnell, but no money was allocated. The Trustees of Captain Cook's Landing Place Reserve pushed for such a road in 1910, but without result. In 1920 the State Minister for Works, proposing a National Museum at Kurnell, also urged a start on a road because weather made the La Perouse-Kurnell ferry crossing unreliable, but his government declined to finance it. Kurnell residents, facing stalemate, felt compelled to act. They were fed up with the 'road' they had themselves built, for it was little more than a fair-weather track.

The residents worked to better define their track in an effort to persuade the government to finance and assist with the construction of a permanent carriageway. Councillor Arthur Hand of Sutherland Shire Council organised a group of six men to take the first motor vehicle to Kurnell on 21st July 1927. Driving a 1919 model Ford which had been converted to a flat tray truck loaded with logs, shovels and chains, the group took two hours to cover the seven miles from Cronulla to Cook's Landing Place. The party included Messrs Bert Saint (the driver), H. Saint, E. G. Vincent, C. Morgan, E. Wells and L. J. Spinks.

The car bogged and sank several times, often up to its axles in the sand or the swamps, but it was recovered safely on each occasion. At Kurnell the mud-smothered party was welcomed by Messrs Coates, Butterworth, Cox (postmaster), Jones (headmaster of the school) and pupils.

The local *Guardian* newspaper reported that on 21st July 1927 history was made when the first car was driven to Kurnell. It is pictured here at Captain Cook's Landing Place. *Dr G.K. Vincent*

As a result of this adventurous journey, Council furnished details and applied for financial assistance from the State and Commonwealth Governments to construct a road 331 chains long. It offered £3,300 from Council's slender funds. But the submission was rejected.

In 1929 the Public Works Department offered a loan of £5000 for the road, intending to use unemployed labour to build it. But Council was unable to fund the balance. Then in 1933 Councillor Joe Monro (the man whose single vote had lost Council the 700 acres of sandhills), newly elected to the Legislative Assembly, proposed that the area between Cronulla and Kurnell be established as a Nature Reserve. The Minister for Lands investigated the proposal and suggested that the entire peninsula be a National Park. The road and the National Park schemes were, however, both rejected by the Government. In January 1935 Surveyor Hill surveyed a route for the road from Cronulla to Kurnell; but still it was not built. In 1936 with the 150th Celebrations approaching, the need for a road to Kurnell became more urgent. Monro, though by then retired from Council, continued to push for a road.

On the 2nd March 1945, a party of MPs, Council officers and others, on board a tabletop truck, traversed the seven miles of quagmire and sand that lay between Cronulla and Kurnell, where they boarded the La Perouse ferry and returned to Sydney. Unfortunately, their considered opinion was that the construction of the road was a low priority, though the MPs did ask Council to submit a road proposal to the Department of Main Roads and to ask for funding. In 1947 drifting sand studies were done. Council calculated that if it were to resume, subdivide and sell the land between Bate Bay and Kurnell as modern residential blocks, the money from the sale could go towards building the road.

In 1948 Stan Latta set about creating a useable road for his bus to Kurnell. He had formerly worked for T. E. Breen, the sandmining and landfill company, so with the assistance of machinery borrowed from Breen and with ashes from the Breen landfill stockpile Latta, together with George Blundell and other Kurnell residents, laid a fairly solid road bed through a stretch of swamp and sand.

Stan Latta, using a loader borrowed from Breen, loading ashes into George Blundell's blitz wagon for the formation of a solid road base, 1947. *GEORGE BLUNDELL*

Kurnell residents building their own road across the sandhills, 1947. *George Blundell*

On 30th April 1949, for the nation's 150th Celebrations, 500 visitors came to Kurnell by boat and by ferry from La Perouse. During the crossing the wind rose and the rains teemed down. The wind, indeed, was gauged at above 60 mph. The Governor could not get within a mile of the site. Arrival by ferry was impossible. He was obliged to return to La Perouse – but the ceremonies went on without him! At the conclusion of the festivities Kurnell was left with over 500 visitors who could not get home. Residents, however, rose to the occasion, fed them, and offered accommodation. Locals shuttled some visitors by truck (which they had adapted to their sandy track) to Cronulla, cheerfully interrupting the arduous journey to rescue and recover RAAF trucks that had become bogged while coming to the rescue of the stranded visitors.

## Taxi Services
A few Kurnell people fortunate enough to own a horse-drawn carriage and with time to spare, operated taxi services for the convenience of local residents. Bullis Jones used his dray, pulled by a retired racehorse. Mr Beaumaker used a converted car-wheeled cart as a taxi.

## On The Buses
In January 1947, Stanley Richard Latta commenced Route 64 with M/O 063, a 1928 model eight-seater American Stutz car. He thrashed the Stutz through the sand and swamps until August 1947 when he purchased a 1928 Rio, a 21-seater bus, from the Kogarah Bus Service. A later bus was a Bedford. These first vehicles were conventional rear-wheel drive.

Ruth Jacobs recollects: 'Mr Cortese had a horse and cart from Cronulla before the Latta's bus. My father, Stanley Richard Latta, had the bus run. He was called Dickie Latta. There was a lot of controversy about bringing the bus through properties to Kurnell at first, but Dad started the motor bus. They put a gate across there where the oyster leases were at Weeney Bay.

Mr Beaumaker and his horse-drawn taxi near the Dampier Street wharf on Prince Charles Parade. Beaumaker also used this vehicle as Kurnell's first fire brigade. *FRED BELL*

'He used to drive the Stutz out here (to Kurnell), pick people up, and take them in to Cronulla to the pictures on a Wednesday and a Saturday night. The Friday night bus was called the 'drunks bus' because it ran at closing time for the pub. Then he bought an old army blitz and they had to drive that out there when the tides were very high because they couldn't get the bus through. And if they did have the bus, they used to have to take the blitz truck too, to tow the bus through the high water. He also used the blitz to carry shellgrit. It was amazing what they did do!

'He kept a shovel behind the driver's seat and chains and planks in the bus. When the bus got stuck it was everybody out, shovel the sand and push the bus out. That was two or three times each trip on route 64. When they put the track through, dad carried the rocks in his truck over the sandhills and helped make the road so the bus could get through without getting bogged. The Kurnell fellas all got in and helped make that little track through the sandhills so that the bus could get through. It was all sand.

'Well, they used to come down that hill and come around the Bay, and of course, when the big high tide came that part of the track used to be under water. And there was an old shack out there and an old chap hung himself in that. And I used to be terrified of going back by there; they used to say there was a ghost

112

Bob Emslie pointing, an irate Dick Latta with a gun, at the Cudgery gate on the road to Kurnell. Latta is endeavoring to stop people using the road. Unauthorised vehicles using the road he had personally made were taking little care of their driving techniques and were cutting the road up and not doing anything towards its upkeep. Nor did the Council do anything. The car is a Hupmobile. *NOLA LATTA*

there. Dad passed away when he was about 52 or 53, so my brother Stan took it over.'

Negotiation and pleas for a substantial road to Kurnell went unheeded, so Stan decorated M/O 305 with flags and signs and drove it around in protest. Though Stan's push for the road fell on deaf ears, the prospect of success loomed from another quarter. Caltex was coming.

*Left.* The blitz wagon that Latta used as his first bus had a canvas cover and seats in the back. *Right.* A later bus is seen here at Cudgery Swamp. *NOLA LATTA*

Stan Latta decorated M/O 305 with bunting and a canvas sign protesting about the lack of a formal road to Kurnell. *NOLA LATTA*

Pryor's Hardware from Cronulla used its delivery truck for a bus on the return run from Kurnell. *SUTHERLAND LIBRARY*

Several years prior to the construction of the Caltex/Council road to Kurnell and for many years after, Spencer Lowe, proprietor of the Alexandria Bus Company, ran a tourist service to Kurnell. Aware that conventional rearwheel-drive vehicles were impractical in the Kurnell terrain, he had a purpose-built coach built on the chassis of a two and a half ton, 6 wheel-drive ex-army GMC

Route 64 followed the track around the Weeney Bay side of Cudgery Swamp where a stone retaining wall attempted to hold back the tides. *NOLA LATTA*

cargo truck. It had a 36-horse power engine. He extended the wheelbase to 19 feet 9 inches, added double wheels to each of the two rear axles, fitted bar-tread tyres to all wheels and raised the ground clearance of the vehicle. The finished cream-coloured coach was 32 feet 9 inches long with a 40-seat passenger body. It negotiated the sand and swamp by engaging the 10-wheel-drive transmission.

The 10-wheel-drive Spencer Lowe GMC coach. *RAYMOND BODDENBERG*

It was claimed to be the largest touring vehicle in NSW and required 4 steps to enter the dust-proofed seating area, upholstered with blue seats. A public address system, a shovel and mattock were available for emergencies.

## Getting on with the Road

In 1950 the Captain Cook's Landing Place Road Trust applied for assistance to build the road. Council, on 30th October the same year, dedicated a strip of land 80 feet wide for the road to Kurnell and named it 'The Captain Cook Drive'. Another three years elapsed before the road was begun. In 1953, Caltex Oil Refinery paid Sutherland Council £50,000 towards its construction and Council added a £30,000 Federal Aid Grant it had received. On Saturday, 28th February 1953, the State Premier, Mr J.J. Cahill, driving a bulldozer, turned the first sod at the Cronulla end, adjacent to the entrance to Towra Point.

The construction of the road was no mean feat. Teams worked from both the Cronulla and the Kurnell ends, laboriously making their way towards a central meeting point. Apart from bush, bogs and sand, the workmen had to contend with the mosquitoes and the snakes, both of which appeared in large numbers. Four months after turning the first sod the unsealed, unfinished road was open to traffic, though work on some parts was continuing.

There was controversy over the thickness of the roadbed. Caltex complained that Council was making it too thick, doing too good a job, costing too much money… these and other points caused work to stop on a number of occasions. Following a legal conference, the original agreement was cancelled and a new

The sod- turning ceremony on 28th February 1953. Pictured on the dais for the ceremony, on what is now the Charlotte Breen Memorial Park, are Premier J.J. Cahill (standing), Shire President Cr D. Welch (to Premier's left), State Member T. Dalton (far left), Federal Member E.G. Whitlam (to Premier's right) and former Shire Presidents Seymour Shaw and Joe Monro.
SUTHERLAND LIBRARY

View of the construction of the road to Kurnell, 1953. Swamps, sandhills, snakes and mosquitoes all had to be negotiated. *Sutherland Library*

one was drawn up that required Council to complete the road by August 1954. Caltex limited its financial contribution to what it had already paid, being the sum of £155,956. Federal Aid Grants covered the balance. The final cost of the road was £181,456. At the end of July 1954, the road opened to all traffic.

## Cape Bailey Lighthouse

The bomboras – treacherous wave actions above submerged reefs – at Merries Reef off Boat Harbour, Point Long Nose, Cape Banks, Bare Island and near Inscription Point had caused the loss of several ships and a great number of pleasure craft, resulting in the deaths of several people. In 1979 the wreck of the *Woniora* was found in waters off Kurnell; it had sunk in 1882. The first warship lost in Australian waters was wrecked and sank after coming to grief on the Cape Banks reef in the 1940s.

A lighthouse was plainly needed because of the nature of the coastline and the many dangerous bomboras. Cape Bailey on the easternmost projection of the Kurnell Peninsula, one and three quarter miles south of Cape Solander at the entrance to Botany Bay, was selected by the Department of Works as the midpoint between Wollongong lighthouse and South Head lighthouse at the entrance to Sydney Harbour.

Work commenced in 1950 and was completed before the end of that exceptionally wet year. Difficulties were, not surprisingly, encountered bringing in the construction materials to the site through the swamps and sandhills.

The unmanned Cape Bailey lighthouse is a square concrete tower standing 180 feet above sea level. Its white flashing light is visible from 25km out to sea. The lighthouse uses a simple but effective mechanism for turning the gas light on

*Left.* The blitz wagon carrying materials to the lighthouse site. *Right.* Building contractor, Keith Golding, beginning the foundations of the lighthouse. GEORGE BLUNDELL

*Left.* Preparing the formwork for the second stage. *Right.* Scaffolding and a crane for raising materials. GEORGE BLUNDELL

*Left.* Lifting a wheelbarrow of cement. *Right.* Inspector from Department of Works (left), George Blundell (front), Keith Golding (right). GEORGE BLUNDELL

at night and off in the daylight. It has a sun valve, an aluminium rod that acts in a similar fashion to a thermostatic switch. When the day cools, the rod contracts and turns on the light; when the sun warms the morning, the rod expands and turns it off. The light is fuelled from bottled gas.

The Cape Bailey Lighthouse completed at the end of 1950. *GEORGE BLUNDELL*

Cape Bailey Lighthouse, 1999.

## Seaplanes

Between 1946 and 1950 it was proposed that the Department of Civil Aviation establish a flying boat base at Kurnell for service between Botany Bay and Sydney. Although the base was never set up, seaplanes did occasionally land in Botany Bay, in front of Alpha House.

Seaplane landing on Botany Bay in 1948. *ELSIE POPPLEWELL*

Seaplane landing on the bay in front of Alpha House at Kurnell, 1948. *ELSIE POPPLEWELL*

## Kurnell Rural Bush Fire Brigade

The first bush fire brigade in Kurnell was a small horse-drawn tender driven in the 1920s by local horse taxi driver, Mr Beaumaker, with his wife as his assistant. Unfortunately there are few records. Floods during the 1974 storms left a foot of water in the headquarters: the cupboard in which the records were kept filled with water and despite futile attempts to save them they were beyond salvage. Fortunately, Nick Boes, one of the members of the Brigade from 1958, is proud to tell of their efforts. Kurnell Bush Fire Brigade was regarded as one of the best in the state. It was held up as an example for others in Sutherland Shire. It has an impressive record of Firsts. Kurnell Bush Fire Brigade rewrote the fire-fighting

Kurnell's pride, after commissioning in August 1966: left to right, Tony Unt (captain), Kon Phillips (in driver's seat), Nick Boes (senior deputy captain), Frank Dixie and John Stenner. *Nick Boes*

Rear view of bush fire tender. *Nick Boes*

constitution. It banned members from wearing inadequate footwear and introduced mandatory boots and overalls for all its fire fighters. Intense community support and fund-raising allowed them to purchase a GMC 6 wheel-drive Army truck that they rebuilt and equipped specifically for their purpose. This truck was the pride of Kurnell, and the State Bush Fire Bulletin acknowledged it as such in a lengthy article that detailed and praised the Brigade's efforts.

## Weather Watching

In March 1999, the Bureau of Meteorology installed an automatic weather station on Sydney Water land beside the reservoir on Kurnell headland.

Most of Sydney's severe weather approaches from the southwest or the south. Kurnell, close to sea level and with an uninterrupted view of the horizon, was chosen for the Doppler Weather Radar installation to provide maximum warning of adverse weather to the heavily populated Sydney region.

This Kurnell installation is a meteorological instrument that continuously monitors rainfall and wind fields within approximately 150 km of Kurnell, with greatest detail closer to the installation. The radar emits electromagnetic radiation which is directed upwards into the atmosphere and the information is transferred via telephone line twenty-four hours a day to weather forecasters who use the information for short-range weather forecasting and warning purposes. Identification of severe thunderstorm activity, including information on squall lines and hail, is foremost amongst these activities, although the strength and timing of arrival of southerly busters that periodically affect the Sydney coast can also be determined. Sea breezes too, and other wind changes, are monitored.

The average television set produces a radiation level of 0.3 microWatts per sq cm (Australian Radiation Laboratories figure). Comparing the Kurnell doppler weather radar to a television set shows that the weather-watch radar radiation at ground level is considerably less than that of the average television set.

The Kurnell electromagnetic doppler weather radar installation, built in March 1999. DAPHNE SALT

# 9 The Village Grows Up

## Early Years

From the earliest days of Sydney's growth, its need of building materials impacted on Kurnell Peninsula. Trees from the peninsula went into housing and bridges. The shell of the large mud oysters in Botany Bay provided lime for mortar, so shellgetters put up shacks around Weeney, Quibray and Woolooware Bays. The impressive number of fish in the bays also attracted fishermen to set up semi-permanent camps. Yet because of the lack of road access, permanent settlers were few in the early years. In 1850 it was reported in the *St George Call* that blacks were more numerous than whites. A village of Kurnell emerged slowly, almost exclusively as a fishing village, and some of its inhabitants were reputed to be refugees from the law. Botany Bay was the highway to the villagers.

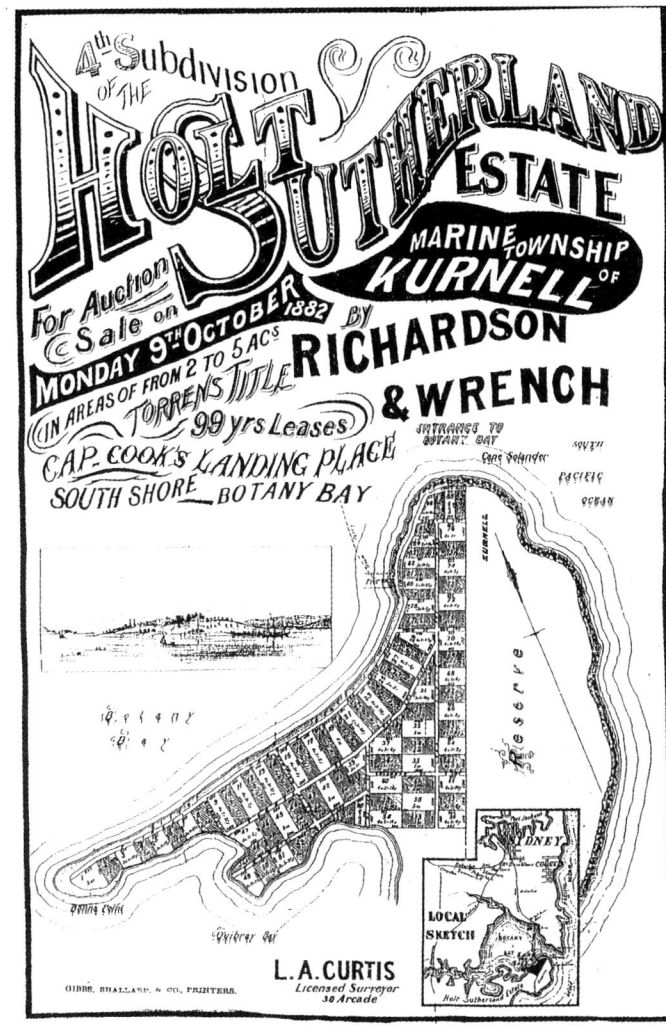

The first subdivision of Kurnell, 1882. *SUTHERLAND LIBRARY*

123

Obelisk decorated for the 1921 celebrations. *MAUREEN BROWN*

Large crowd at Kurnell for the 1939 Cook Landing Celebrations. *HARRY MORGAN*

On Monday 9th October 1882 Richardson and Wrench auctioned a subdivision of the Holt Sutherland Estate, termed pretentiously 'The Marine Township of Kurnell'. Many of the blocks were absurdly narrow with 21-foot and 22-foot frontages, justified on the grounds that Kurnell Village was projected as a Fishing and Holiday Resort. The blocks were considered to be adequate for weekenders. But the frontages were soon found to be too narrow for permanent residents; so blocks were coupled to make 42-foot and 44-foot frontages.

Kurnell had been a tourist and holiday destination for many years. Sir Joseph Carruthers in the 1880s and 1890s frequented the region for its fishing and shooting. The historic significance of Captain Cook's Landing Place was recognised and the annual landing celebrations persisted.

But until Council and Caltex built the road, the isolated village of Kurnell had a closer relationship with La Perouse and Botany than with Sutherland Shire.

In 1925 Kurnell's isolation prompted the residents to attempt to form their own municipality; but the Minister for Local Government refused to accede to their entreaty and the residents were left pretty much to their own devices. Kurnell 'just growed up'. During the 1930s Depression a 'Happy Valley' of fishing and holiday camps sprang up around the peninsula with settlers paying the landowners a fee for permissive occupancy. Building components for the homes were gleaned from the bushland or improvised from scrap, empty containers, abandoned items, and materials brought over by boat from La Perouse, Botany or Sans Souci. The ferrymen also carried foodstuffs, newspapers and household goods for the settlers.

Bringing building materials up from the boats. *Sutherland Library*

## Early Dwellings

Most of the dwellings were little more than shanties, but the ingenuity of the settlers was often evident. Typically, swamp oaks were cut on Bonna Point and on the site of the present oil refinery. Residents lashed the stakes together and covered them with split hessian bags or kerosene tins. The hessian was whitewashed to render it waterproof, while internally the walls were lined with newspapers. Kerosene tins, their ends removed, were flattened out to give a sizable sheet of steel, used mainly for nailing to the exterior. Most of the floors were of stamped dirt.

During the 1950s, after the road from Cronulla to Kurnell had been constructed, a great number of second-hand houses were brought to Kurnell on trucks from other places in Sutherland Shire to provide inexpensive homes.

The Watson residence in Bridges Street Kurnell was typical of early homes in 1920s. *HARRY MORGAN*

'Glencoe', 1930s, stood on what is now vacant land beside the shopping centre in Torres Street. *HARRY MORGAN*

The Cox hessian home, 1918, with Ann, Bert and May Cox seated by the door,. *HARRY MORGAN*

*Left.* House being moved from South Cronulla. *Right.* Being placed on its new location in Bridges Street, Kurnell. *GEORGE BLUNDELL*

## Village Life

After the First World War, Kurnell village began to take shape, replacing the 'shanty town' of fishing shacks and holiday camps. It was a small, peaceful hamlet and attracted retired and unemployed folk. The main settlement areas were around the waterways. Regular dances were held in the Cox general store each Saturday night and in Guy's Hall on holiday weekends and special occasions; and later in Marton Hall. The Village of Kurnell was officially proclaimed in the Government Gazette of November 1933.

Between the wars and until the early 1950s, Kurnell boasted an open-air theatre. Lee Jones recalls: 'We used to go down to the Open Air Theatre in Cook

Part of Kurnell Village from the roof of the Kurnella Café, looking southeast, 1952. *George Blundell*

Street, a little to the left of the Caltex cutting. On rainy nights we'd sit there in raincoats, our rubber boots on and our umbrellas up. The ground could be covered in water but we would stay and watch the movie out. It was lovely on a

Aerial view of Kurnell in the 1920s, showing Captain Cook Landing Place Reserve and the Reserve wharf in the foreground, Kurnell village is facing Botany Bay, and the dairy on what is now Caltex Oil Refinery in the upper right. *Sutherland Library*

Aerial view of Kurnell in 1999. Captain Cook Landing Place Reserve and Alpha House in the foreground, Kurnell Village facing Botany Bay, Towra Point in the upper right. The Reserve wharf, seen in the previous photograph, was demolished by the 1974 storms. Caltex wharf and the sand-stabilising groynes jut out into Botany Bay from Silver Beach. *DAPHNE SALT*

nice summer's night, if you didn't mind the mosquitoes and sandflies. It was fun sitting there looking at the stars on the screen and in the sky.

'Where 'Eze by the Bay' is now, (on the corner of Prince Charles Parade and Polo Street) was vacant land. Occasionally we had a special night's treat. Free movies! So people brought their chairs, pillows, blankets and kids and settled in for a pleasant night's viewing. Now and then the wind came up and blew the screen away and everyone scrambled back to their camps.

'After this theatre closed, the Saturday night bus used to take us in to Cronulla. There was no road of course, and the bus would get bogged two or three times a trip. The driver would shout, 'All out!' – everybody would have to push the bus, you know. I must admit that if it was raining it was the gentlemen who ended up at the theatre wet, not the ladies!'

Tea Trees grew along the foreshores of Silver Beach until the 1950s. This native plant belongs to the *Myrtle* family; its leaves have been used at times for brewing tea, but it is for its aroma and the aromatic oil in the leaves that it is valued. ELSIE POPPLEWELL

## Commercial Enterprises

The first store opened in Kurnell in 1918 on the corner of Polo and Cook Streets. The proprietors, Bert and Ann Cox, erected a hessian chaff bag shelter painted with whitewash to keep the water out and they put in it a trestle table as the counter.

Kurnell's first store was opened in 1918 by the Cox family, on the corner of Polo and Cook Streets. HARRY MORGAN

Inside the Cox hessian store in 1918, a trestle table served as the counter. *Harry Morgan*

Palmer's store and Post Office, 1919, was set further back on the same block of land as the present Post Office and Village Store. *Sutherland Library*

Mr and Mrs Palmer had let a room or two of their home as a boarding establishment since 1912. In 1919 they converted the front rooms of their house to form the first solid Kurnell shop. It incorporated a Post Office.

Following the tragic drowning of Harry Palmer in Botany Bay in 1920, Mrs Jenny Cox bought the Palmer Store and Post Office from his widow. Adjoining

General store section of the Cox store was the original Palmer shop. *HARRY MORGAN*

The Post Office section of the Kurnell shopping complex 1924. *HARRY MORGAN*

Ann Cox collecting the daily mail from the ferry, 1944. *Harry Morgan*

the Cox family home on Bonna Point was a separate corrugated iron building that they used as the master bedroom. Because of their concern for the education of the children, it was in this room that they began to teach their own and other local children. After they had purchased the Palmer Store, the Coxes loaded this structure onto a four-wheeled dray, brought it down to the shop and attached it to the existing building. This became the Post Office section, creating an 'L' shaped building.

Jack Honnor was a builder and entrepreneur. With his wife and children he moved to Kurnell about 1916. The Honnors bought several blocks of land between Prince Charles Parade and Torres Street. The northern end of Torres Street is now part of Captain Cook Drive. There was a vacant block of land between their home, 'Gymea', and their grocery shop. The shop was gutted by fire in the 1940s. Honnor made the bricks he used to build his houses, his shop, Bob Mackie's Maritime Museum and the Methodist Church.

Mr Pillinger had a small paper shop and general store where Sydney Diver City Guided Underwater Tours now stands. It was called the corner shop, not because it was on a corner, but because it was then the shop closest to the corner.

Mr Stillwell, who had the dairy on the ocean side of the refinery site, also had a market garden. He sold his produce to the people of Kurnell from his horse-drawn dray.

Mrs Guy's shop and her function hall, known as Guy's Hall, stood between Dampier Street and Balboa Street, facing the bay. She catered to the villagers' need for recreation, showing movies, and holding dances on most weekends and holidays. Ever enterprising, she installed an ice-cream making machine to the

The Honnor shop was opposite the now refinery wharf on Prince Charles Parade. The site is vacant Caltex land today. *ELSIE POPPLEWELL*

The Kurnella Café 1947 during its construction. *GEORGE BLUNDELL*

Interior of the Kurnella Café; scales for the general store rest on the counter. GEORGE BLUNDELL.

delight of the children. Guy's Hall was demolished in the 1970s, but the 'dunny' (outhouse) was retained as a garden shed.

During the late 1940s Rube Chater, the builder who built the present Marton Hall, had a bake-house on Prince Charles Parade.

Gus Sprague was the son of Mrs Guy. He built a weatherboard general store on the southern side of Polo Street on the bay side of the park entrance. The shop was sold to Mr Cortese, who later sold it to Robert Emslie. In 1947 Emslie built a semi-circular façade around the old edifice, using bricks made by Ivy Martin

The Kurnella Café/service station 1954, George Blundell's pre Blitz Austin A70 utility beside fuel pump. GEORGE BLUNDELL

Blundell's first Blitz in front of the Kurnella Café, 1948. *George Blundell*

and her husband in their backyard. He demolished the inside of the original building and refurbished it. The building was then named Kurnella Café.

The Café was a general store with a restaurant and petrol pumps. The Blundells managed the business with Jessie Blundell and Ethel Emslie serving in the shop and cooking for the restaurant. Celestine and Harold Stevens baked the

The Official Opening in 1953 of the Caltex garage. A tabletop was put on the hoist in the lube bay for the occasion that was attended by officials from the new Caltex refinery and by Shire councillors. *George Blundell*

Up to the mid 1950s, nearly all of Sydney's suburbs had a 'Milko', with his horse-drawn milk cart and Kurnell was no exception. *FRED BELL*

Fred Bell, Kurnell's 'Bottlo', collected empty bottles to recycle them. He still lives in the village. *FRED BELL*

pies sold there. The Kurnella Café had the first liquor licence in Kurnell and so was able to serve liquor with meals.

George Blundell, who operated the service station in conjunction with the business, did most of the deliveries and collecting of supplies, first with an Austin A70 utility, then with an old ex-army short wheelbase blitz wagon he had bought in 1947. He kept the decrepit old blitz for about a year before buying a bigger one from the army disposal yards at Tempe. It was almost brand new, with an army canopy and high sides, which he removed in order to convert to an eight-foot by eighteen-foot flatbed tray.

In 1951 Blundell operated a sawmill in the oak forest on his father-in-law's land between Stillwell's dairy and Solander Street.

There was still no water or electricity to Kurnell, so Robert Emslie installed his own diesel-engine generating plant in a separate brick building. It operated 24 hours a day for seven days a week till the power came through in 1952. It was used to run the refrigeration, lighting and other power needs in the shop. In 1959 Emslie sold the business to Alan Columbo who continued the restaurant for a while as 'Cook's Kitchen' before demolishing the building when clientele fell off. He retained the liquor licence, which he transferred to a new liquor shop. The land is still a vacant block.

Following the establishment of the Caltex refinery at Kurnell, George Blundell was the first manager of the first and only service station in Kurnell. It opened in 1954. George kept the garage until October 1956 when he sold out to Maurice Appleby.

## School Days

As the village of Kurnell evolved and the numbers of children increased, parents showed great concern for their education. The isolation of Kurnell from the rest of Sutherland Shire for lack of a road had prompted the Cox family to take the problem in hand.

They started the first school in Kurnell in 1918 – in the bedroom of their family home on Bonna Point, between Balboa Street and Guy's Hall. The Department of Public Instruction had set land aside for a school in Dampier Street and began a provisional school in 1921; but a permanent school was not built until August 1923.

The 1921 single room provisional school was on the same site as the present school. *FRED BELL.*

Fun in the schoolyard. Clearly, no one wore shoes to school! *Fred Bell*

Alf Jacobs recalls: 'In the 1930s there was about 20–26 kids in the one room school. John Roach was a nice bloke for a teacher. When we found out that he'd died we all went to the funeral there. He was pretty flamin' strict, but 'e was doin' the right thing, makin' sure we was all right. We 'ad a spellin' competition once a week. I never ever got anythin' spelt correctly! One week he read the tests and read them again and said, 'Well that does it, everybody pack up and go home, you all got every word spelt right!' It was the only time that ever 'appened! The kids from here used to go by ferry to Botany for their immunisations, and we had to go over on the ferry to Maroubra for high school. (The children crossed the bay to attend high school at Maroubra, Kensington or Long Bay.) At one stage, before the drainage was put down, there was a huge puddle in the middle of Torres Street. Old Alf Bundy would get his little rowboat and row the children from one side to the other side to get to the school.'

Wandering stock left to graze on the Kurnell Peninsula on agistment became a problem for the residents. (Agistment fees were paid to the Trustees of the Reserve.) On one occasion a straying bull became aggressive and was tearing around the schoolyard, threatening the children. Bob Grant, the park ranger, was called in to shoot the unfortunate animal.

## Kurnell Individuals

Mention must be made of some special individuals who have contributed to Kurnell's history.

Claude Marquet was a well-known political cartoonist who expressed a radical philosophy and an idealistic view of the worker in his cartoons. In 1914

CLAUDE MARQUET.
(By Himself.)

*Left.* Marquet's caption: 'Patriotism Should Begin at Home. The Anniversary of Australia's Birthday has again passed practically unnoticed – Unpatriotic Fact'. *Right.* Self-portrait. titled, 'Claude Marquet, by himself'. *CAROLINE DAVIS*

Claude and his wife Ann built a home at Kurnell. In April 1920 he and Harry Palmer (grocer of Kurnell) were returning to Kurnell in Claude's sailing boat, which was filled with household and shop supplies, when they were overwhelmed by a sudden squall. Their boat was discovered anchored in Botany Bay, still filled with groceries, but with no sign of life on board. Their bodies were never recovered. The boat was later auctioned.

John Weir with his children on the BSA Bantam bike. *CAROLINE (WEIR) DAVIS*

*Left.* Weir in his backyard, 1962. *Right.* Weir and Jenni Booth (Davis) 1997. CAROLINE DAVIS

In July 1920 a memorial book was published in Claude Marquet's honour. Proceeds of the sale were given to his widow. Many of his friends including Henry Lawson, then living in the Sutherland Shire at Como, penned memorials in the book.

No chronicle of Kurnell can be complete without mention of John Graham Weir. John and his wife settled permanently in a Kurnell fishing cottage. Turning his hand to many things, he fished, harvested seaweed, organically grew vegetables, milked cows for his neighbours and began a poultry farm, all the time working at the Bunnerong Power House and commuting on his BSA Bantam motor bike.

He later went to work as Public Relations Officer at AOR and threw himself into community work in his spare time. He wrote and produced the *Kurnell Village Newsletter* on an old gestetner copier and then personally delivered it. For more than 25 years he was President of the Kurnell Progress Association and involved in most other local community organisations. In 1970 he received

Polo Street, 1950, from front of the Kurnella Café looking east to Thieves Hill. GEORGE BLUNDELL

Sutherland Shire Council's first Citizen of the Year Award, and in 1971 was further recognised with an MBE for his community work. From 1971 to 1974 he served as an Independent Councillor on the Council. As this book goes to press, the Kurnell Progress Association is dedicating a park for the community as the John Graham Weir Memorial Park. He died in March 1998.

Kurnell is home to some well-known and talented artists, such as Otto Kuster, whose works hang in galleries and homes throughout the world.

There were many 'characters' in the village. 'German Bob' lived on what was called Thieves Hill, in Polo Street, where he grew grapes and made wine, though he never drank himself. The locals exchanged fish and garden produce for the wine. Bob also distilled perfume from grevillea flowers, selling it in Sydney where he went to play his trombone in the Prince Edward Theatre.

'King George', who always walked around in a trench coat, was viewed as a rough diamond, but he appears never to have done anything but mind his own business, which was often simply fishing.

'Metho May' also lived on Thieves Hill. Everybody was terrified of her. She died doing a high dive off the bridge to Bare Island, La Perouse – it was low tide and she had dived onto rocks!

'Little Freddie' claimed to have a birthday every weekend. He wore his old felt hat pulled down over his face and would always go down to meet the Sunday ferry. He walked among the visitors and said to them, 'It's my birthday'. They would give him a few coins; so the little scoundrel saw to it that he did indeed have a birthday every weekend.

Kurnell resident, Robert (Bob) Mackie, a journalist and cartoonist, wrote and published *The Sentinel* newspaper, *Who's Who in Business in the Sutherland Shire,* and *Pacific Portal.* In 1956 he wrote and published the *Golden Jubilee of the*

Today the old village camaraderie is still evident. Fred Bell, 'Bottlo' since he was 15 years old is seen here taking Santa Claus (June Jacobs) around Kurnell at Christmas time to give sweets and other small gifts to the children. In recent years the Kurnell Rural Bushfire Brigade has taken over Fred's Christmas rounds. *FRED BELL*

Some of the exhibits in the grounds at the entrance to the Nautical Museum at Kurnell. Sometimes while Mr Mackie was explaining the specimens in his collection, his wife told fortunes for the ladies by reading their tealeaves as she extended her hospitality over a 'cuppa'. SUTHERLAND LIBRARY

*Sutherland Shire* from his Caringbah newspaper office. Mackie was an insatiable collector of unusual, nautical and Cook-related artifacts. So extensive was his collection that public-spirited Bob opened a museum in the 1940s near the Roman Catholic Church on Prince Charles Parade. He decorated the exterior of a shed with old oil company signs such as Mobil Pegasus, Standard Oil, Golden Fleece and Purr Pull. Inside his 'Captain Cook's Australian Museum' he had such items as Aboriginal weapons, early newspapers and cartoons, a series of British, German and Japanese helmets dating back more than 100 years, a 'genuine Crusader's helmet 700 years old', and another which he reckoned to be a 1300 year old Roman helmet. There were newspaper clippings about Cook's voyages, memorabilia from the early days of the Sutherland Shire, and a model of the *Endeavour.* Bob offered to sell the museum to Sutherland Shire Council, which showed little interest, and the museum was taken over in 1958 by Stan Unwin, hitherto a dealer in old wares.

Unwin added to the collection and maintained the decrepit look of the building. He also extended it using flattened kerosene tins for the cladding.

Even before one entered the property, it was said, 'you got your money's worth by reading the signs'. His charges: *Single Adults – 2 shillings; Man and Wife – 3 shillings; Man, Wife, 1 children – 3 shillings; Man Wife 2 children – 1 shilling and 6 pence.* The more children you had the cheaper it became! A lateral thinker, he told a friend on the quiet that the shed and most of everything came from the tip; yet of anything that looked remotely nautical or doubtful he would say, 'Yes that's definitely a Captain Cook relic!' He had all manner of specimens – odd, unusual, unique, natural and not so natural – mostly displayed in glass jars. When the museum closed, the National Parks and Wildlife Service took its contents to the NPWS Discovery Centre for critical examination. The building, an eyesore, was then demolished and the land left vacant.

## Places Of Worship

**Methodist.** Mr Honnor built the brick and concrete Harold Wheen Memorial Methodist Church using cement bricks he had made himself. Rev Harold Wheen laid the foundation stone on Australia Day 1927. The President of the Methodist Conference, Rev. F. J. Hynes, opened it on 21st May 1927 and Rev. J. G. Wheen gave the address. The church had a seating capacity of 80, but by the 1980s there were rarely more than 25-30 attending worship. It was put up for auction on 15th February 1986 and is now a private home.

**Anglican.** The foundation stone was laid in January 1927 and the church was officially opened in April of that year. Thirty years later there was a need for a larger building to house the congregation; so the old Anglican Church building from Cronulla was moved to Kurnell in the early 1950s. In 1960 St James Church of England built a new church and hall.

**Roman Catholic.** The foundation stone was laid on 14th November 1937; the St John Fisher Roman Catholic Church was officially opened and blessed by Cardinal Gilroy in March 1938. The priest crossed the bay by ferry on a Saturday night for the occasion, sleeping in the church so that he would be ready for Sunday's early morning Mass. Kurnell is now part of the Cronulla parish.

**Baptist.** In September 1960 the Baptists of Kurnell began to hold their services in Marton Hall. They built their own church in 1966.

## Marton Park

With the interests of the young people at heart, the Kurnell Progress Association approached Sutherland Council with a proposition for setting aside some land for a playground. In 1945 Council acquired a triangular shaped block of marshland between Captain Cook Drive, Solander Street and Cook Street, and reclaimed a portion of it by draining it and filling it with rubble and soil. In conjunction with the Captain Cook Landing Place Trust commemoration of the anniversary of Cook's birth, the playing field was dedicated and named Marton Park, after Captain Cook's birthplace, by Justice Ferguson on 27th October 1951.

## Kurnell Progress Association

Kurnell Progress Association was formed in December 1909. In 1918 Ann and Bert Cox made a room in their home available for the meetings. In 1920 the Progress Association met in Guy's Hall on the corner of Dampier and Prince

Members of the Progress Association laying the Foundation Stone for Marton Hall, 1952. The hall, however, was not built around this stone. *Harry Morgan*

Charles Parade. Frank Cortese, who built and owned the Kurnella Café, was a President during the 1940s. John Graham Weir was President for 25 years from 1959.

In 1952, this active Progress Association laid the Foundation Stone for a Community Centre to be named Marton Hall, after the Estate in England on which stood the two-roomed thatch-roofed cottage in which Captain Cook was born.

Cook's birthplace in England, marked by a memorial urn. In the background may be seen the remains of the original Marton Hall, which was destroyed by fire in 1960. Photographed in 1995. *Daphne Salt*

However, the hall as planned was not built, for Caltex Oil Refinery donated a shed and put it on land a little further back from the Foundation Stone. This provisional, ready-made hall was later converted for their needs as the village function centre by the local citizens, using materials supplied by Sutherland Shire Council. It was lined and painted inside and on one wall hung a beautiful tapestry displaying the Lord's Prayer. The Hall was officially opened in January 1953. But this position of Marton Hall proved to be inconvenient, so it was moved and re-erected with some modifications in March 1956. Only four months later it was again changed, this time by turning it around to face Captain Cook Drive. A Baby Health Centre and a doctor's surgery were established within Marton Hall and in 1959 a licence was granted to screen films.

Unfortunately, in November 1967 a fire caused by an electrical fault destroyed the hall. All records and the tapestry were lost. Ironically, Marton Hall in England too had been lost to fire.

Disappointed but not disillusioned, the residents built the present Marton Hall, a substantial structure, which was officially opened by Councillor Ray Thorburn in November 1968.

The Progress Association, which has evolved into today's Kurnell Progress and Precinct Committee, continues its battles against ever-encroaching industry and its campaigns for safety, environmental protection and community amenities.

A sample of relatively recent achievements of the Kurnell Progress and Precinct Committee:

- Re-commencement in 1995 of the annual Captain Cook Landing Anniversary re-enactment, festival and art show.

A choral function in Kurnell's first Marton Hall, 1950s. *SUTHERLAND LIBRARY*

The *New Endeavour* in Botany Bay for the Captain Cook Landing Anniversary, 1995. *Betty Jacobs*

- A NO STOPPING sign erected at the school.
- Major road and traffic improvements including a roundabout on the corner of Torres Street and Captain Cook Drive.
- Bicycle track along Captain Cook Drive.
- A 60 kph sign on Captain Cook Drive.
- Scholarships for school students.
- Weekly clean up of Silver Beach.
- Some current projects of the Kurnell Progress and Precinct Committee:

The *New Endeavour* sails into Botany Bay in 1998 for the Cook Landing re-enactment. *Noeline Thomas*

- Dedication of the John Graham Weir Memorial Park. A successful appeal to the Department of Urban Affairs resulted in council handing over a block of land for this purpose. Fundraising hopes to provide the means for erection of a suitably inscribed bronze plaque that will be fixed to a rock and surrounded by a semi-enclosed paved seating area.
- An *Adopt Kurnell Historic Drive* project to rejuvenate, improve and clean up the 'lifeline' to Kurnell – Captain Cook Drive.
- An avenue of the flags of all nations, flying for the year 2000 Olympic Torch Relay.
- Save Towra Point and create a walkway through the Towra Wetlands; and a walkway through the wetlands behind Marton Park.
- Creation of an impressive entry to Kurnell Village – tree-planting etc.
- Improvements to Silver Beach and provision of benches and seats.
- Provision of bus shelters, kerb and guttering throughout Kurnell.
- Beautification of all of the Peninsula's industrial landscapes.
- Recommencement of the ferry run to Kurnell as a permanent service.

## Kurnell Sport and Recreation Club

Caltex commenced this club in 1953 as a recreational facility for its workers. Ladies were later permitted to use it but for many years were not admitted as members. In 1978 Caltex handed the facility over to the village as a general community club. Today the club has several affiliated clubs and community facilities within it.

Aerial view of Marton Park, November 1999, showing Marton Hall, Stingrays Football clubhouse and oval, netball and tennis courts, playground, garden and the pre-school. A creek and wetlands surround the park. DAPHNE SALT

## Kurnell Community Youth Development Committee

On 1st September 1999, representatives from Kurnell Stingrays Club, Kurnell Netball Club, Kurnell Nippers Club, Kurnell Girl Guides, Kurnell Scouts, Kurnell Tennis Club and Kurnell Progress and Precinct Committee met to devise common projects for the benefit of the youth in Kurnell. As a result of this meeting, the newly formed committee is investigating the viability of developing the wetlands behind Marton Park and building a multi-purpose track and heritage walk around the park. The walk, an environmental experience, is to include viewing platforms over wetlands and will feature displays of both Aboriginal and white history of the area.

## Kurnell Stingrays Club

The Kurnell Junior Rugby League Football Club was formed after a committee meeting on 17th November 1991. In all, seven teams took to the field for the 1992 season. The clubhouse, built in Marton Park adjacent to Marton Hall, caters to an active membership in excess of 180, including players. Today the Stingrays are fielding ten teams in competition with other clubs. The name 'Stingrays' originates from Cook's own log when he first named Botany Bay 'Stingray Harbour'. The Kurnell Stingrays are currently attempting to raise funds to buy equipment for the youth in Kurnell and investigating the possibility of installing a running track for training purposes around the football oval.

## Kurnell Catamaran Club

Formed in 1971, in an ex-army shed carted to the site, this club built a clubhouse and later extended and renovated it with the voluntary labour of the members. Races are held every Sunday on Botany Bay.

Dianne Miller and Kevin Thomas are sailing their catamaran. *NOELINE THOMAS*

## Community Organisations

Kurnell, a village with its own identity and sense of guardianship, has had many active community groups and organisations associated with it:

Visitors to Kurnell on Good Friday 1906. Photographed at Inscription Point. *MITCHELL LIBRARY*

- **Botany Bay Field Studies Centre and The Discovery Centre.** Both are housed in a complex in Botany Bay National Park, Kurnell, under the administration of the of National Parks and Wildlife Service which works closely with the Kurnell community.

- **Coast and Wetland Society.** Formerly the Littoral Society, it has identified at Kurnell some of the few freshwater habitats in the Sydney region available to several bird species, especially migratory species, and is fighting to protect and manage them as a freshwater wetland complex.

- **Cronulla Dunes and Wetland Alliance.** Fights for the preservation of the unique and delicate ecosystems of Kurnell Peninsula.

- **Dune Care.** The State has, through municipal councils, an organisation known as Bush Care. The Kurnell branch of this is widely known as Dune Care and holds fortnightly working parties.

- **Early Childhood Centre.** Provides a good start for pre-schoolers.

- **Friends of Towra.** Works to clear the weeds from Towra Reserve and safeguard its shoreline and wetlands.

- **Kurnell Catamaran Club.** For leisure and pleasure on Botany Bay.

- **Kurnell Community Sports and Recreation Club.** Provides an organised and constructive outlet for the energies of young people.

- **Kurnell Musical Society.** For the melodious edification of all.

- **Kurnell Pensioner Club.** An active group of senior citizens with a pride in their village.

- **Kurnell Progress and Precinct Committee.** Dedicated to the advancement, recognition and protection of Kurnell Peninsula.

- **Kurnell Pre-School Kindergarten.** Built with a generous donation from Calsil Bricks.

- **Kurnell Public School.** Built in 1923.

For the 1999 Captain Cook Landing Anniversary Festival a special ferry service ran hourly from Kurnell to La Perouse. The catamaran, *That's Life*, is seen here taking on and discharging passengers at the temporary Kurnell wharf.

- **Kurnell Regional Environment Planning Council** (KREPC). Formed in 1998 by representatives of ten groups and working with them to achieve rehabilitation of the peninsula.

- **Kurnell Residents Against Cogeneration Establishment** (RACE). Formed to resist location of a large energy plant within the boundaries of the Caltex Refinery.

- **Kurnell Tourism Committee.** Working to achieve a great tourist future for 'The Birthplace of Australia'.

- **M.U.C.K.** (Mothers Unite in Care for Kurnell). A dedicated action group which has fought many environmental battles for Kurnell; for example, against unwanted industry on the peninsula.

- **Music Museum.** Bob McDonald rebuilds and restores musical instruments.

- **North Cronulla Precinct Committee.** One of Sutherland Shire's most active precinct committees; it bridges the interests of Cronulla and those of Kurnell Peninsula.

- **Potter Point Upgrade Committee.** Striving for rehabilitation of this once beautiful area, ravaged in recent decades by sewerage activities.

- **Shepherd Academy of Dance.** For the constructive graceful expenditure of energy.

- **Sutherland Shire Environment Centre.** Through concern with the whole Shire, the Centre is involved at many points with the peninsula's rehabilitation and is a member of KREPC.

# Appendix

There is confusion about Captain James Cook's actual landing date. Some records state that he landed at Kurnell on 28th April 1770, others that he landed on 29th April 1770. Both dates are correct!

In Cook's own handwriting in the *Endeavour's* ships log, his landing is recorded on Sunday 29th April. Cook wrote: 'In the PM …Anchor'd under the southern shore about 2 Mile within the entrence in 6 fathoms water … as we approached the shore they all made off except two men who seemd resolved to oppose our landing … I fired a musket between the two … one of them took up a stone and threw at us which caused my fireing a second Musquet load with small shott … Emmidiatly after this we landed…'

However in the *Endeavour* Journal of Joseph Banks on April 28th 1770 Banks writes: 'After dinner the boats were mann'd and we set out from the ship intending to land … two men came down … each armed with a lance … in all appearances resolvd to dispute our landing to the utmost'.

In the official log of the *Endeavour,* Cook is using the naval ships' dating. In ships' time the journal day begins and ends at 12 midday. Hence an entry for April 29th begins with the events of the afternoon of the previous day, and concludes with the morning of the date written on the page. Cook used ship's time and Banks, being a civilian, wrote his entries using the civilian calendar time.

We can further add to the confusion if we take into account that Cook did not make any adjustments for crossing and re-crossing the International Date Line until October 1770 when he reached Indonesia. He wrote the date in his journal, thus: 'Wednesday 10th October according to our reckoning, but by the people here Thursday 11th'. If we take this into account, any dates for Cook and Banks along the coast of Australia should be adjusted by another day – making the calendar date of 28th April really the 29th!

Thomas Luny's impression of the *Earl of Pembroke,* which was renamed *Endeavour Bark,* in Whitby Harbour prior to departure for London and Plymouth. NATIONAL GALLERY, CANBERA.

# References

*A Pictorial History of the Sutherland Shire,* Joan Lawrence, Kingsclear Books, 1997.

*Aboriginal Technology – Some Evidence from the Kurnell Peninsula,* F.P. Dickson 1968.

*An Energetic Colonist, A Bibliographical Account of the Activities of the late Hon Thomas Holt MLC,* Henry E. Holt, Hawthorn Press, Melbourne 1972.

*An Historical Work on Australasian Discovery and Colonisation,* Henry William Hemsworth Huntington, August 29th 1855.

*Ancient River Systems of Botany Bay,* A.D.Albani, P.C.Rickwood, B.D.Johnson, J.W.Tayton. *Antiquity publication* 1968

*Chronicle of Australia 1993,* Chronicle Australasia Pty Ltd Ringwood, Victoria.

*Classic of Shan Hai,* written in China before 338BC.

*Dedication of Captain Cook's Landing Place Kurnell,* Botany Bay, Department of Lands 1899.

*Department of Mineral Resources Records Geological Survey,* Vol.20 Part 2, pp. 159-250.

*Dinkum Aussie Bicentenary,* Bob Ryan, Child & Associates Publishing 1988.

*EIS on H1,* Woolooware Bay Kurnell, March 1982, Donges & Assoc.

*EIS July 1997,* prepared for Sithe Energies Australia Pty Ltd, Woodward-Clyde Pty Ltd.

*Environment Australia,* Biodiversity.

*Excavation of Midden Boat Harbour February 1974 for Director NPWS,* F.P. Dickson, University of NSW.

*Excavation of Midden Boat Harbour, Kurnell, During August 1971 for Director NPWS,* F.P. Dickson, University of NSW.

*First 50 years of the Sutherland Shire Council 1906-1956,* David Kirkby (original manuscript & Sails to Atoms).

*From Causeway to Clubhouse* 1991 Daphne Salt

*Gas Exchange in the Roots of Mangroves,* P. F. Dam, L. van Scholander 1955.

*Gateway to the South, An Intimate insight into the Origins of the Sutherland Shire,* Daphne Salt, 1987.

*Geography and Geology, Aboriginal Archaeology of the Sutherland Shire,* D.F. Branagan.

*Holocene Geological Evolution of the Southern Botany Bay-Kurnell Region,* O.S. Roy & E.A. Crawford, January 1979.

*Illustrated History of the Sutherland Shire, Birthplace of a Nation,* Fred Midgley, Southland Historical Press, Sutherland ,1969.

*In the Footsteps of Captain Cook,* Tom Kenny, 1000 copies published by J.C. Trenear, Tempe.

*Interim Report by D.N. Foster University of NSW Water Research Laboratory 1974.*

*Journal of a Voyage to New South Wales,* John White, Surgeon General to the First Fleet and Settlement at Port Jackson, Originally published 1790. With bibliographical introduction by Rex Rienits, edited by Alec H. Chisolm, Published in association with RAHS by Angus and Robertson 1962.

*Kurnell – The Birthplace of Australian History,* Immigration and Tourist Bureau, April 1909.

*Kurnell Development Control Plan,* Planning & Environment Commission of NSW - Sutherland Shire Council, October 1980, Cameron McNamara Pty Ltd.

*Kurnell Peninsula Development Study,* Kurnell Peninsula Planning Study, August 1979, Paul Landa, Minister for Planning & Environment.

*Martha Matilda of Sydney Town (Wife of Captain James Birnie of Alpha Farm, Kurnell)*, M. Hutton Neve, Sutherland Shire Historical Society 1972.

*Oyster Culture on the Georges River, New South Wales*, T. C. Roughley 1922.

*River, Road and Rail,* Kogarah Municipal Council 1985.

*Sutherland Estate Report 14th April 1868,* Robert Cooper Walker.

*Sutherland Shire – A History to 1939,* Maryanne Larkin, Sutherland History Press 1998.

*Sutherland Shire Historical Society Bulletins.*

*Sydney's First Years,* Reprint of a Narrative of the Expedition to Botany Bay and A Complete Account of the Settlement of Port Jackson, Captain Watkins Tench of the Marines, published by Angus & Robertson in association with the Royal Australian Historical Society 1961, 1962.

*The History of Botany Bay 1788 – 1970,* Captain Cook Bicentenary 1770 – 1970, Frederick A. Lancombe, for the Council of the Municipality of Botany 1963.

*The James COOKbook, Captain James Cook 1728 – 1799, His Recipe of Life,* 1996 manuscript, Daphne Salt.

*The State of the Bay: Botany Bay 1998,*Garry Smith, internet site.

*The Voyage of Governor Phillip to Botany Bay,* originally published 1789, in association with the RAHS by Angus and Robertson 1970.

*Towra Point Nature Reserve Draft Plan of Management,* Towra Point Steering Committee, Bernie Clarke (Botany Bay Planning and Protection Council), P. Medway (Friends of Towra Point Nature Reserve), P. Adam (Coastal Wetlands Society), L. Thorburn (Environment Australia),S. Black (NSW Waterways Authority), M. Matchett, P. Rougellis (NSW Ministry for Forests and Marine Administration), M. Way (National Parks Association), A. Smith, J. Hannan (NSW Fisheries), P. Stevens, P. Shadie, G. Ross, J. Erskine, G. Dunnett (NPWS) 1999.

*Toxic Cities and the fight to save the Kurnell Peninsula,* Garry J. Smith 1990, New South Wales University Press.

*Trial Excavations in Captain Cook's Landing Place Reserve, Kurnell NSW,* J.V.S. Megaw, Senior Lecturer, Department of Archaeology, University of Sydney 1968, University of New South Wales Department of Industrial Arts.

*Two Hundred Years in Retrospect: Kurnell – Sutherland 1770–1970,* John Walker 1970.

*W.B Ullathorne,* 1868 Autobiography.


## Newspapers, Magazines & Periodicals

*Mankind* magazine July 1931, J.S. Rolfe, December 1931.

*People* Magazine 11th September 1963, pages 12 – 14, article by Jeff Carter.

*Sydney Morning Herald* 8/5/1899, p4, Aboriginal Place Names by Frederick Samuel Ellis Holt.

*SMH* 17th January 1856, 26th June 1856, 1st Govt land sale Sutherland district.

*SMH* 8th July 1867, Holt & his grass.

*SMH* 26th January 1863, People 24th February 1865, Daily Mirror 2nd May 1860, timber & the Drain in Woolooware Bay.

*SMH* 10/8/1881 Princes George and Albert planted pine 4 trees, 2 were Araucaria Cookii.

*SMH* 4th December 1873 Holt's concern at logging.

*SMH* 24/5/61, p.5, Tabbigai, Kurnell cliff dwellers 25/5/61 p.2; 8/6/61 p.2; 9/6/61 p.2, 7; 21/6/61 p8; 16/8/69 p.16.

*Pix/People* 14/3/74, Vol 9 No.3, p.17 story by Thompson.

*St. George & Sutherland Shire Leader,* 24/11/65 p.6; 21/12/66 p9; 23/7/69 p.3.

## Individuals

I sincerely thank each of you who have contributed information about Kurnell, shared your knowledge and experiences, allowed me to copy your photographs, and assisted me in many other ways.

Allen, Margaret
Annesley, Michael
Armstrong, Joy
Audet, Gwen
Barrack, Lillias
Bell, Fred
Birtles, Cathy
Blundell, George
Boddenberg, Raymond
Boes, Nick
Bollins, Frank
Booth, Graeme
Boulton, Marg
Bourke, Kevin
Brown, Maureen
Buckley, Bruce
Bussing, Lenie
Campbell, Don
Clarke, Bernie OAM
Cogan, Joyce & Ray
Curby, Pauline
Curtis, George
Davis/ Weir, Caroline
Delmas, Norman
Dever, Robyn
Dunnett, Gary

Exon, Dorothy
Fernandez, Skip
Gietzelt, Arthur
Gordon, Ian
Gormley, Jenni
Griffiths, Aileen OAM
Hannan, Patricia
Hedison, John
Hiskins, Stan
Hogan, Annette
Holt, Chris
Holt, Phillip
Hume, Jean
Jacobs Betty and Alf
Jacobs, June
Jacobs, Ruth & Bert
Jones, Lee and John
Kimberley, Simon
Lagos, Margo
Larkin, Maryanne
Latta, Nola
Lord, Pat
Marshall, Bill
Martin, Clive
McDonald, Helen
McGrath, Alan

McNally, Peter
McWilliams, Pete
Morgan, Harry
Morgan, Phil and Alfred Henry
Murray, Pat
O'Halloran, Bill
Parr, Phil
Popplewell /Honnor, Elsie
Risbridger, Ross
Scott, Jan
Skinner, Alice
Sloan, Jim
Sparkes, Gwen
Stevens, Margaret
Thomas, Noeline
Timbery-Beller, Beryl
Vincent, Dr G. K.
Vissar, Julia
Walshe, Bob OAM
Wheeler, Dorothy
Whitlam, E, Gough
Williams, Iris
Williams, Shayne

# Index